Conducting

an

Amateur Orchestra

MALCOLM H. HOLMES

DEAN, NEW ENGLAND CONSERVATORY OF MUSIC

HARVARD UNIVERSITY PRESS

CAMBRIDGE · MASSACHUSETTS

1951

CONDUCTING
AN AMATEUR ORCHESTRA

To Sir Adrian Boult, in friendship

ACKNOWLEDGMENT

MY thanks go to Dr. Archibald T. Davison for his painstaking reading of the manuscript and his thoughtful suggestions for its improvement; to Mrs. Raphael Demos, head of the Department of English, New England Conservatory of Music, for her helpful structural criticisms; and to Paul Chancellor, Margaret Clark, Ruth McGregor, Dorothy Little, and Harold Sproul of the Greenwood Music Camp faculty, who acted as a board of consultants for the first two drafts. I am deeply indebted to the several college generations of Harvard, Radcliffe, and Wellesley students I was privileged to conduct. They really wrote this book for me.

M. H. H.

CONTENTS

FOREWORD, by Archibald T. Davison   xi

INTRODUCTION   1

I   AUDITIONS   9

II   SEATING THE ORCHESTRA   18

III   PROGRAM BUILDING   28

IV   REHEARSAL PLANNING   39

V   DETAILED REHEARSALS   46

VI   THE FINAL REHEARSALS   58

VII   THE CONCERT   70

VIII   ORCHESTRAL BASIC TRAINING   80

IX   ORGANIZATION   87

X   SIGHT READING   93

XI   ADDITIONAL SOURCES OF ORCHESTRAL REPERTORY   103

XII   CODA: SECONDARY SCHOOL—COLLEGE—COMMUNITY   110

APPENDIX

Partial Repertoire: Harvard Orchestra, 1933–1942   119

Partial Repertoire: New England Conservatory Orchestra, 1945–1950   123

FOREWORD

THE mere announcement of the publication of this book will have, for many, an almost apocalyptic significance: alike to those who feel that they were born to the conductor's ermine, but who, when faced with the opportunity of putting their powers to the test, find themselves ignorant of the most elementary procedures of conducting; and to those harried souls, like school music teachers and idealistically minded community leaders, who have had the task of training an orchestra thrust upon them.

These, however, are but two among many interested groups of readers who will find here valuable instruction and advice. I am thinking particularly of one class of musicians who, either through choice or restricting circumstance, have enjoyed a conducting experience confined to the chorus. Sooner or later fate overtakes them; the occasion arises when they must assemble an orchestra and train it to play accompaniments, shall we say, to choral works. Accustomed to attacks obtained by the provocatively lifted eyebrow and the vaguely beckoning gesture, they are dismayed to discover that their initial motions invoke only silence or, at most, musical chaos. The shock is painful and enduring; when at last something like coherent sound emerges, the relieved tyro beats on and on, dreamily aware that everything is wrong but nervously overjoyed that in some magical way he has set the ether astirring. Resolutely he rejects the idea of stopping, because if he did call a halt he would have no notion of how to set things right, and worse, there would be the disastrous prospect of having to get the music started all over again. At such moments a composite picture of all the neatly tailored titans of the podium flashes across his beleagured consciousness, and he fervently and wisely determines to explore well the lower slopes of Parnassus before again attempting the ascent.

To anyone whose concern is the conducting of an amateur orchestra this book will offer much valuable information: to the discouraged beginner who has forgotten that before the soaring butterfly comes the earthbound chrysalis; to those of moderate experience; and to the seasoned workman who will find it a most useful handbook of orchestral procedure. Malcolm Holmes, whose wizardry in converting orchestral amateurism into near-professional competence never ceases to amaze, is just the man to have written this work. He cannot, to be sure, make you an orchestral conductor, but he can tell you and has told you what you ought to know about this enthralling occupation.

ARCHIBALD T. DAVISON

CONDUCTING
AN AMATEUR ORCHESTRA

INTRODUCTION

THIS book is intended as a guide for conductors and prospective conductors of amateur orchestras of every type: elementary school, high school, preparatory school, college, and community. Its objectives are threefold: (1) to suggest methods of dealing with the various problems connected with the establishment, maintenance, and development of a good amateur orchestra; (2) to discuss the major technical difficulties involved in training amateurs, and the means for surmounting them; (3) to outline ways of enlarging the amateur orchestra repertory by drawing on little-explored sources of material of the highest standards, ideally suited to the needs of the groups under discussion.

The techniques described here have been evolved over a span of twenty years with the stimulating coöperation, one might even say guidance, of the orchestras I have been privileged to conduct at Harvard, Radcliffe, and Wellesley colleges, the Concord Summer School of Music, the Berkshire Music Center, the New England Conservatory of Music, the Greenwood Music Camp, and the Harvard Musical Association. Not a few of these techniques have been shaped by the penetrating wisdom and sympathetic understanding of Sir Adrian Boult. Others are the result of contacts with the instrumental work being done in schools, colleges, and communities in Massachusetts and New York through guest conducting, adjudicating, and observation.

At the outset, it must be made clear that it is impossible to reduce the conducting of amateurs to an exact science and to state categorically that this or that procedure is a foolproof formula guaranteed to produce a good amateur orchestra. There are too many variable factors and intangibles involved. In this very fact lies the source of the intense personal satisfaction and stimulation the individual conductor can, and should, derive from working with and for amateurs.

There are really as many different ways of developing and training a good amateur orchestra as there are conductors. Personality alone could account for this diversity. Conductor A may have such a command of himself and his players that he can make a success of a technique which might fail utterly if borrowed intact by Conductor B. In addition, there is the further complication that no two amateur orchestras have the same composite personality and no two, therefore, can be handled in exactly the same way. For example, the same training techniques cannot be applied successfully to a group of men, a group of women, a mixed group, or a group of children without modifications and adaptations to fit the needs of each. It is true that the fundamentals remain the same, but the methods of applying them do not. The conductor must constantly analyze the results of his training to make certain that he is meeting the needs of his players.

The techniques set down here are, therefore, really in the nature of tested guides which may need to be adapted to meet the requirements of the particular orchestra involved, usually through a process of trial and error. They must also be tailored to fit the conducting style and personality of the individual conductor, for he must make any technique completely his own if it is to have the conviction necessary for success with his players.

I have already used the word "good" several times in describing the sort of amateur orchestra in which I am interested. There is no such thing as a bad amateur orchestra. Inept or unimaginative leadership will produce one in short order, but the fault lies with the conductor and not with the players. It is impossible for the conductor to be a success and the orchestra a failure. Most of the blame for a poor concert by an amateur group must rest with the conductor, because the responsibility for faulty training or for the overambitious choice of program material is inescapably his. It is indeed unfortunate that lapses along these two lines have caused the word "amateur," at least in its musical connotation, to become a synonym for dilettante mediocrity.

To develop a good amateur orchestra, the conductor must have had sufficient training and experience in the mechanics of his art to enable him to teach his players, collectively and individually, to realize to the fullest their potentialities of the moment. The key word in the preceding sentence is "teach." The conductor of an amateur group must be a teacher in the finest sense of the word, for the material with which he has to work is seldom expert enough to produce the desired musical effects without detailed technical advice. The conductor's equipment must, therefore, consist of far more than beautiful hands, long wavy hair, and a good tailor. Furthermore, in choosing the music for his programs the conductor must be willing to subordinate his own personal ambitions to a careful and searching analysis of the technical and aesthetic capabilities of the orchestra.

Last, but far from least, the conductor must possess sufficient *savoir-faire,* through natural gift, study, or experience, to enable him to strike a happy medium between Simon Legree and Little Lord Fauntleroy in handling his players.

There are many divergent views concerning what constitutes the proper basic training for an orchestral conductor. The following list of subjects is, of course, designed for those who expect to work primarily with amateurs. Some of the subjects are best taken as organized courses at the college or conservatory level; others may as profitably be explored by the individual with the aid of a good textbook. No attempt has been made to draw up this list in any arbitrary order of importance:

Orchestral Conducting: Extensive training in the mechanics of conducting, supplemented by practical experience with a laboratory orchestra.

Score Reading: Ability to read and master scores of all periods, styles, and degrees of complexity.

Instrumentation: A complete general knowledge of all orchestral instruments and an intensive practical knowledge of at least one string and one wind instrument. The knowledge of a string instrument is of vital importance in working with amateurs.

Piano: At least a working knowledge of the keyboard. The additional ability to play from open score would be an invaluable asset.

Solfège: Training sufficient to develop an acute ear for pitch deviations, and the ability to master whatever rhythmic problems the conductor may have to solve for his players.

History of Music: A general survey course, including analysis of form.

Harmony and Counterpoint: Sufficient knowledge to enable the conductor to detect mistakes in scores and parts, to serve as an aid to score reading, and to facilitate the making of musically literate arrangements for whatever combination of instruments he may have at his disposal.

Interpretation: A knowledge of the re-creative process, which is perhaps best learned through the intensive study of an instrument, supplemented by personal observation and study of the methods of leading conductors and performing artists, by reading, and by the study of records.

In addition, it is to the prospective orchestral conductor's advantage to have at least a basic knowledge of choral conducting as a preparation for possible later collaboration with a school or community chorus. This will also serve as a supplement to his study of orchestral conducting, for instrumental phrasing stems from vocal —to mention but one example—and the knowledge of methods of voice production will help in his own singing illustrations.

A knowledge of the fundamentals of psychology would also be helpful.

There is no substitute for practical experience. The ideal way to obtain it is through a season or two of training as assistant to an established conductor. Such a procedure will afford ample opportunity for intensive observation, for actual conducting under supervision, and for developing one's own orchestral technique.

The conductor assumes a great responsibility when he takes over the direction of an amateur orchestra, a responsibility which goes deeper and reaches further than is apparent on the surface. His main task is, of course, to produce the finest orchestral results that time, patience, effort, and the available instrumental material will permit. He must also increase the orchestra's prestige and enlarge the scope of its artistic contribution to the school or the community. He must constantly stimulate local interest in orchestral music and in orchestral instruments so that his group will increase in size and musical stature as time goes on. To these ends, he must secure the co-operation and active support of the musically-minded adult public.

All of these primary objectives are important, but there is an even greater responsibility inherent in the conductor's leadership. He should always seek to enrich the musical lives of his players and his audiences by bringing them into close contact with the finest music from every period. His choice of program material must conform to the highest and most uncompromising standards in order to raise the level of orchestral performance and of audience appreciation.

These two elements are vital needs in the amateur field at the present time. We may be proud that the performing standards of the major symphony orchestras of America are the highest in the world today but we cannot honestly feel the same about the accomplishments of our semiprofessional and amateur orchestras.

The reasons can be traced back to the imperfections in the early instrumental training of children and the general inadequacy of the teaching and orchestral material to which they are first exposed. There is often, on one hand, too casual a choice of the private teacher without benefit of expert guidance or advice; on the other, an unfortunate tendency on the part of the teacher and the conductor to give children music that is termed "good enough" when the very best is needed. In the critical formative years, the combination of poor private teaching, poor teaching material, and the use of indifferent orchestral literature induces aesthetic anemia. An appalling amount of natural musical talent is lost or has its growth stunted before it has a chance to develop.

The conductor of the amateur orchestra, faced with the handicap of having to work with players indifferently or poorly grounded in fundamentals and brought up under inadequate standards of music selection, must utilize every opportunity to improve the situation in his community by seeing to it that his players study with teachers of proved experience and ability whose musical taste is both broad and sound.

In the meantime, there is much that he can do in his own particular province. First, he can raise the standards of his orchestral repertory and broaden its scope, and in so doing develop and improve the musical intelligence of both his players and his audiences. This is important because our listening standards, which have an interlocking effect on performing standards, are far below what they should be. American audiences are too easily hypnotized by flashy renditions of musical shoddy and are far too tolerant of indifferent performances of masterworks. We accord the same thunderous reception to good and bad music and to good and bad playing.

Second, the orchestral-training program must seek a broader motivation than the necessity for preparing the next concert. The conductor should always bear in mind that he is working with two types of players: those who may go on to make music a profession, and those who will find in music, through listening or performing as amateurs, a source of personal enjoyment and relaxation. His mission with the former is to ground them thoroughly in the art of orchestral playing in order that they will have the preparation necessary to qualify them for admission to a conservatory and eventually for a professional career; with the latter, to prepare them for participation in further amateur ensemble work and for a lifetime of intelligent listening in the concert hall.

This preparation at the successive educational levels determines, to a large degree, how successful the individual will be in whatever he chooses to do with his talent. The conductor of the amateur orchestra must, therefore, concern himself not only with the present but also with the future of his players if he is to discharge his full responsibility.

The greatest satisfaction one can have from working in an art comes from the opportunity to help others develop the talent which has been given them. In this sense, the conductor of the amateur group is more strategically placed than his professional colleague. From his painstaking work should come the replacements for the professional orchestras as well as the intelligent and informed listeners who are the potential supporters of every form of musical endeavor. A conductor could ask for no greater challenge.

I

AUDITIONS

THE purposes of the audition are (1) to determine which of the candidates for admission to the orchestra are qualified to meet its performing standards; (2) to obtain an over-all estimate of the ability of the new orchestral material, upon which to base an efficient and equitable seating plan; and (3) to discover any remediable defects or imperfections in the individual instruments, and to obtain information regarding the quality of each of the latter.

The audition procedures outlined in this chapter are based on the assumption that sufficient orchestral material is available to justify the institution of a selective process for membership in the orchestra. If the amount of material is limited, the conductor may find it expedient to modify, or even postpone, the suggested exhaustive audition until he has been able to stimulate more interest in instrumental music in general and in the orchestra in particular. In such cases, the establishment of definitive auditions for membership should be one of his first objectives. For obvious reasons, it is not feasible to hold auditions for orchestras composed of students of elementary school age. Here the conductor should consult with the private teacher to ascertain whether or not the student is sufficiently advanced to profit from membership in an orchestra.

The audition serves as more than a source of information for the conductor. First, it provides the individual player with a goal and incentive for his practice. Second, it gives prestige to the successful applicants, and indirectly to the orchestra, when membership is on a competitive basis. Needless to say, players will not value membership in an orchestra whose criteria for admission are the mere possession of an instrument and the physical ability to transport it as far as the rehearsal hall. Last, but far from least, the competitive audition relieves the conductor from the extraneous pressure too often brought to bear on behalf of players of dubious musical attainments but of impeccable antecedents.

By one means or another, the exact nature of the audition should be communicated, in advance, to the prospective candidates. It is important that they should be freed of the psychological handicap of not knowing what is to be expected of them. They should also be given the opportunity to prepare themselves as adequately as possible. Ample publicity in the local or school press is but one way to advertise the auditions. To supplement this by holding some pre-audition musical or social gathering is most valuable as a means of making it possible for the candidates to meet the conductor and the other members of the audition committee, and of giving the prospective new members some idea of the performing capacity that will be expected of them. All this will inevitably help to lessen the tension caused by the audition.

For example, the Harvard University Orchestra holds a sight-reading evening just prior to the auditions, to which all students who play orchestral instruments are invited. This is not a rehearsal as such, but an informal evening of reading at sight from the standard orchestral literature. During the intermission, the president of the orchestra tells the candidates something about the history and organization of the group. This is always an interesting feature, as the Harvard Orchestra was founded in 1808 and is the oldest orchestra in the country, antedating the New York Philharmonic-Symphony Society by thirty-four years. The conductor explains the forthcoming auditions in detail, outlines concert plans, and describes the prospective repertory for the year. The evening ends with refreshments, and during this period the conductor, officers, and old members of the orchestra make a point of meeting the candidates and of making them feel at home.

By the time such an evening is over, the candidates will have had a chance to become acquainted with the aims and ambitions of the orchestra as well as with its officers and members. They will know what they can expect of it in a musical and social way and what it will expect of them. The orchestra may even win over a student or two who previously doubted his ability to carry a full scholastic program and participate in an extracurricular activity at the same time.

The Radcliffe College Orchestra holds a luncheon, and the Wellesley College Orchestra, a tea, at which essentially the same procedures are followed. At both of these affairs, each of the players and the candidates wears a tag giving her name and instrument to facilitate the process of becoming acquainted.

Informal gatherings such as these not only help to accomplish the purposes for which they are designed, but also serve to impress the prospective members with the fact that the organization is efficient, alive, and worth joining. Since the inauguration of these preliminary meetings, audition grades at the three colleges have improved noticeably.

Wherever possible, the conductor will find it advantageous to choose a committee of officers or section leaders to assist him in hearing the auditions. There are several important reasons for this suggestion: (1) The added responsibility given to an officer or section head helps to build group spirit and morale among the leaders of the orchestra. (2) Each of the applicants is more likely to feel that he has had the fairest possible hearing, no matter what the decision may be in his particular case. (3) The conductor is provided with an advisory board of players experienced in the various orchestral instruments with whom he can check his own judgments in individual cases.

The audition formula I use with students of college age is as follows: (1) scales, both major and minor, diatonic and chromatic; (2) portions of two pieces of the candidate's own choosing, one primarily for tone quality, phrasing, and interpretation, the other for technical facility; (3) unfamiliar passages from the orchestra's standard repertory, to be played at sight.

The player is graded under each of four headings: tone quality, intonation, technical facility, and sight reading. The importance attached to the last of these will, of course, vary according to the age-group involved. Less can be expected of the candidates for elementary and high-school orchestras and more in the case of college and community orchestras.

Before the audition, the candidate fills out the first four items of information on a card such as that reproduced on the opposite page.

HARVARD UNIVERSITY ORCHESTRA

1. Name _____ Address _____

2. Instrument(s) _____ Years of Study ____

3. Experience (orchestra or band) _____

4. Pieces to Be Played _____

5. Tone___Intonation___Technique___Sight Reading___

6. Remarks _____

The grading system is on a basis of 1 to 10, divided as follows: 10, 9.5, and 9, A; 8.5 and 8, B; 7.5 and 7, C; 6.5 and 6, D; below 6, failing.

The highest grade (10) represents the ideal or standard the conductor has established for the orchestra in question. This will naturally vary according to local conditions, the quantity and quality of the available material, and the type of orchestra involved—school, college, or community.

Beginning the audition with scales allows the players to warm up before attempting the more taxing requirements. In the case of the strings, these scales are in two or three octaves starting with G-major for the violins and C-major for the others. The second scale might be A-flat or E-flat (or the relative minors), for the purpose of testing more exhaustively the accuracy of intonation and of exploring the strength or weakness of that usually neglected portion of the string player's anatomy known as the fourth finger. Each scale is played slowly, with vibrato, using the entire bow for each note. In the case of the winds and brasses, the scales cover the entire effective range of the instrument or the player. The addition of a rapid chromatic scale, either legato or tongued, is also suggested for these instruments.

For the second part of the audition, it is seldom necessary to hear more than a portion of each of the two pieces chosen by the candidate to obtain an accurate estimate of his natural ability, degree of advancement, and the efficiency of his practice habits. The conductor and his associates should resign themselves in advance to hearing numerous renditions of the "Meditation" from *Thaïs,* Borowski's "Adoration," Saint-Saën's "The Swan" and the "Carnival of Venice."

As previously stated, the passages for sight reading are chosen from the present or past repertory of the orchestra. The object is not to trip the candidate, but to find out how well he can handle music of the difficulty he will encounter during his membership. The facility with which an amateur orchestra can read over new music has a most important bearing on the degree of success it can hope to attain in its concerts.

The passages chosen include a slow section to test tone quality, phrasing, and innate musicianship, and a fast section to test mechanical facility and coördination between the eye, the brain, and the hands. The player is instructed to observe all the indicated dynamics and phrase markings. For the clarinets, trumpets, and horns, there is at least one passage testing ability to transpose at sight. It is also important to find out whether or not the trombonists can read the alto and tenor clefs.

On the basis of the information obtained from the three divisions of the audition, the conductor and his committee should be able to arrive at a fair and accurate estimate of each player's ability. Here, for example, is a tabulation of the ratings of eight college freshmen violins under this system:

Player	Tone	Technique	Intonation	Reading	Years of Study	Years of Experience
A	9.5	9	9.5	9	11	6
B	9	8.5	8.5	7.5	10	5
C	8	8.5	9	7	7	4
D	8	8	8.5	7	6	4

Players A through D were accepted as first violins.

E	8.5	8	7	7	9	6
F	7.5	7	8	7	7	5
G	7	7	7	6	8	4
H	7	7.5	7	5	6	4

Players E through H were accepted as second violins, with E placed at the first stand. Notice that E qualified as a first violin under this system of grading but was placed at the first stand of seconds for the purpose of strengthening the section. This will be explained in more detail in Chapter II. Candidates whose grades were lower than those of H were rejected in this particular year because the existing vacancies in the two violin sections were then filled and because those below H in the grading did not show sufficient ability to warrant increasing the size of the sections. It is obviously a great mistake to take on players who are not yet ready just for the sake of increasing the size of the orchestra.

Quite often, however, there will be a number of borderline cases which merit special consideration. The grades may lie between 6 and 7 with an occasional failure grade of 5. The causes of the low grades are usually evident at the audition—tenseness beyond the player's control, lack of practice (a common fall ailment following the summer vacation), or insufficient experience and practice in sight reading.

If seats can be found for them in the orchestra, these players are placed in a special category known as "provisionally accepted," with the understanding that they will be given a second audition at the end of one month of attendance at the regular rehearsals of the orchestra. This new audition is based entirely on passages from the works under preparation. In actual practice, a provisionally accepted player will seldom fail to qualify under these favorable conditions. It becomes a matter of pride with him to work hard, both in and outside of rehearsal time, and earn a place as a regular member of the orchestra. In this way, some very usable talent may be salvaged which might be lost permanently if an outright rejection is made at the time of the original audition.

The provisionally accepted group may also include any qualified surplus wind, brass, and percussion players for whom vacancies do not exist because of a wealth of material holding over from the preceding season. These players are permitted to attend scheduled rehearsals and gain orchestral experience by playing along with the regulars by means of a judicious system of doubling of parts or by a certain amount of rotation. These players understand in advance that they will not necessarily appear in the concerts unless a vacancy occurs through illness or withdrawal. The conductor is thus protected against last minute defections in the ranks, and at the same time has an opportunity to train these surplus players as future replacements. If enough surplus material exists, a training orchestra may be formed, under the regular conductor or his assistant, to act as a feeder for the first orchestra.

At the time of the original set of auditions, the conductor makes notes on the quality and condition of the individual instruments. The foundation of good orchestral tone is good instruments in a good state of repair. The attention of the player should be called to such defects as false strings, cracks, wornout bowhair, defective pads, incorrect reeds, faulty mouthpieces, and so on. The conductor must later check and see that the suggested changes or repairs have been made. "The infinite capacity for taking pains" is not only the hallmark of genius, it is also the wall motto of the successful conductor of an amateur musical group.

Repairs and minor mechanical improvements are comparatively easy to make, but the problem presented by the instrument of definitely inferior quality is not so easily solved. To help the player of limited means or to supply the capable player who does not own his own instrument, the conductor must have at his disposal a collection of good instruments. Some schools, colleges, and communities are fortunate enough to own such a collection from which loans can be made to responsible players. If such a collection does not exist, or is inadequate for the orchestra's needs, it should be one of the conductor's first concerns on taking charge of the orchestra. Not even Heifetz can make a factory "Stradivarius" sound well. Every possible source of aid should be investigated: the private donor, the parent-teacher organization, the local men's and women's clubs, the benefit concert, and even the powers-that-be who control the school, college, or community purse strings. There will be an enormous amount of inertia to overcome, so this important campaign must be started early and go hand-in-hand with the development of the orchestra as a worthwhile musical entity.

11

SEATING THE ORCHESTRA

Upon completion of the auditions, the conductor faces the problem of drawing up an efficient and equitable seating plan which will distribute to best advantage the available material, both new and holdover. He must seek to combine the new players with the old, the experienced with the inexperienced, and the aggressive with the passive in such a way that, with intelligent coaching in ensemble playing, a smoothly coördinated musical entity will result. The importance of the seating plan cannot be overemphasized, for it is a vital factor in determining the degree of success the orchestra can hope to attain. A great deal of time, effort, and painstaking care must be devoted to this task, for the results may well mean the difference between mediocrity and competence or between competence and excellence in performance.

The first step in drawing up the seating plan is undoubtedly the easiest, for it is a comparatively simple matter to choose the concertmaster, principal second violin, first viola, first cello, first bass, and the solo winds and brasses. Where there is more than one outstanding candidate available, an open competition is the best solution. In nine cases out of ten, the positions listed above will go to holdover members of the orchestra who have had one or more seasons of experience under the conductor and have proved themselves in public concert. Occasionally a talented newcomer will appear to provide the exception to the rule.

The factors to be considered in seating the remainder of the membership include musical ability, experience, and qualities of leadership. The conductor has obtained evidence at the auditions on at least the first two factors for the new members. Some additional credit for experience should be given to those players who have been in the orchestra for a season or two and are, therefore, acquainted with the conductor's rehearsal methods, beat, and personal eccentricities. Leadership is that almost indefinable quality which expresses itself in the orchestra through a certain incisiveness or aggressiveness of playing. It stems from natural ability, good training, self-confidence, and experience, and distinguishes the leader from the mere follower. It is clearly visible, and audible, from the podium.

For purposes of group and individual morale, length of service in the orchestra should be given some consideration in determining the order of seating, for there should be opportunity for advancement within a section as the individual develops and gains orchestral experience. The burden of proof is on the player himself, however, for an amateur orchestra is no place for the prima donna. The deciding factor in seating must be the good of the group as a whole, not the pride or ambition of the individual—or his parents. To avoid misunderstanding, the conductor must make his policy clear from the outset.

In many cases, the correct solution to the problem of the seating plan is obtained only by means of trial and error. A plan that looks well on paper is not always successful in actual practice. The conductor must not hesitate to make changes if it later appears that his original estimate of the various players was at fault.

The String Sections

The usual solution to the problem of seating the strings is to place the best players at the front desks, with the others trailing off toward the rear of each section in direct descending order of ability and experience, thus:

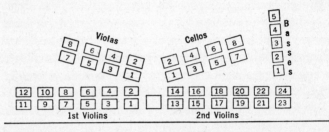

Not only does the curve of musical efficiency drop rapidly toward the back of the sections so arranged, but the conductor's control over each follows the same curve. Throughout the rehearsal period he will be hampered in his efforts to mold each section into a cohesive unit because the most able and experienced players are clustered about the podium where their potentialities of leadership are out of range of those who need them most. It often happens in concerts that these musical suburbs are swept by contagious epidemics of stage fright over which the conductor can have little or no control.

This system has one other major fault: it places the more competent players en masse in the first violin section, while the unfortunate remainder wind up across the railroad tracks as seconds. Here they proceed to bog down in a mass inferiority complex of tremendous proportions. It is this sort of procedure which has given rise to the artificial stigma, both musical and social, now attached to the words "second violin."

An orchestra so constituted in its various string sections should confine itself to simple marches and waltzes of the "Sobre las Olas" type, for its chances of giving adequate performances of good orchestral music are practically nil. Needless to say, the polyphonic music of Bach and Handel is impossible to perform unless the second violins are capable of bearing a melodic and rhythmic burden equal in difficulty to that of the firsts.

It should be obvious that the conductor needs as much control over the back desks of strings as over the front desks. For this purpose, the seating arrangement should be based on the military principle of "strength in depth." Each section should have a spinal column from front to back of experienced players plus those newcomers who seem to possess the qualities of leadership previously mentioned. Sitting with them at the various desks will be the less experienced and less aggressive players who need someone upon whom they can lean. The veteran who can divide his attention skillfully between the printed page and the conductor's beat will carry along the inexperienced player who buries his head in the music and seldom, if ever, comes up for air.

To strengthen this system in the second violins, it is advisable to have at least one player of first violin calibre lead the section. If violin talent is plentiful, it is even better to assign two such players to this important task and have the first desk a truly strong unit. The nature and responsibilities of the assignment will have to be explained to the players chosen because of the afore-mentioned class distinction which exists, and it should be made clear that a job well done will inevitably lead to transfer to the first violin section.

With the first desk problem settled in both violin sections, the remaining players can be seated along the lines just suggested. The following example is a purely fictional one, but will serve to illustrate the procedure:

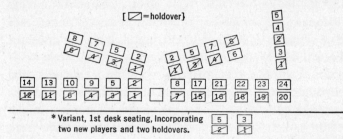

[◹ = holdover}

* Variant, 1st desk seating, Incorporating two new players and two holdovers.

With some degree of equality established between the violin sections, the conductor can foster a certain amount of rivalry between them by having the one illustrate the playing of a given passage for the other. Any device of this sort that the conductor is able to use will help to develop a high level of group spirit and morale within the orchestra which, in turn, will be communicated to the audience through the playing. Without it, the performance of an amateur orchestra can be dull, pedestrian, and lustreless.

Woodwind and Brasses

The seating problem in these two divisions of the orchestra is a comparatively simple one because of the relatively small number of desks and players involved. Not too long ago, one would have had to add "and the smaller number of players available." However, the recent phenomenal growth and development of bands by secondary schools and youth organizations has resulted in a steady flow of experienced wind and brass players into the college and community orchestras. This often means that there are more qualified players than there are vacancies in the orchestra.

At one memorable set of auditions for the Harvard Orchestra, eleven flutes appeared. Of these, five qualified for acceptance with really outstanding performances of such pieces as the Bach B-minor Suite, "L'Apres-midi d'un Faun," and the flute variation from the Brahms Fourth Symphony. As there were two experienced holdovers from the preceding season, this meant that the conductor had seven talented candidates for three regular positions. When this same situation prevails in the clarinet section, one cannot help but wish that there were an orchestral "major league" so that one might trade three flutes, two clarinets, and a sum of cash for a promising oboe or bassoon. Where such a surplus of qualified players exists, it will pay dividends to carry two players on each part, as suggested in Chapter I. In such cases, the first and third players are combined on one part; the second and fourth on the other.

Orchestras lacking a complete instrumentation may find an additional use for surplus wind players by utilizing a flute or a clarinet in place of a missing oboe; or by having a clarinet reinforce a weak or undermanned viola section, or serve as a substitute horn.

One of the primary objectives of any amateur musical group should be to enrich the musical experience of as many qualified persons as come within its orbit. The conductor should make every effort to achieve this end, but without compromising the performing standards of the orchestra.

The addition of a piano as a supplementary instrument in orchestras lacking a complete instrumentation is strongly recommended, at least as a temporary expedient. It is justified wherever its use supplies missing parts or makes available to the small or incomplete orchestra musical material it cannot otherwise perform. The use of saxophones as a stopgap, at least at the college and community level, is not recommended. These instruments, when playing parts not specifically written for them, do not blend well with the general orchestral tone. Many American editions of standard works provide optional saxophone parts, however, which may be used to advantage by school orchestras of limited size.

In closing, it may be well to say a word or two concerning the physical seating of the orchestra on the stage. There are two basic plans to consider. The first of these,

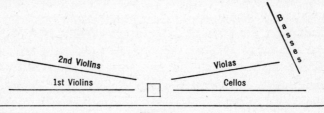

Plan A

Plan A, has the violins together on the conductor's left with the violas, cellos, and basses in one order or another on his right. In the diagram this order is determined by the supposition that the cellos are more numerous than the violas. The advantage of this plan is that it masses the violins in one compact sector with the *f*-holes all pointing out. This results in a cohesive, well-balanced violin tone in all types of orchestral music and in a well-defined interplay of the two most prominent voices in polyphonic music. The disadvantage is that not all amateur orchestras possess sufficient depth of material in the viola, cello, and bass sections to present a balanced stage picture if they are placed on the conductor's right. If this plan is adopted, the section (viola or cello) with the larger number of players should be on the outside nearest the audience.

The other arrangement, Plan B, has the first violins on the conductor's left, the seconds on his right, and provides two possible variants for seating the violas,

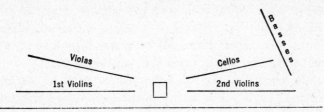

Plan B

cellos, and basses. It has the advantage of balance, at least from the point of view of appearance, and allows the conductor to place the violas on his left, with the *f*-holes pointing out, and so compensate somewhat for their usual numerical inferiority. The disadvantage is that some of the second violin tone is bound to be lost, since it is directed into the body of the orchestra and away from the listener. The conductor working under this plan must constantly strive to counteract this disadvantage by developing a full-bodied tone within the seconds and by urging them to "play out." Only in this way can he prevent the constant give-and-take between the first and second violins from being lost to the listener.

With professional players, the direction of the *f*-holes is a minor matter, but with amateurs it can be of vital importance. The violas are placed on the left in Plan B because of my personal conviction that, in general, the inner voices lend depth and richness to the orchestral tone and, therefore, must be given every chance to be heard.

The seating arrangement adopted will also depend

upon the size and shape of the stage involved. It should not be a fixed matter, as circumstances often dictate changes from year to year, or even from hall to hall.

The winds and brasses should be seated in as compact and self-contained groups as physical conditions permit. The French horns should be close to the woodwinds, and

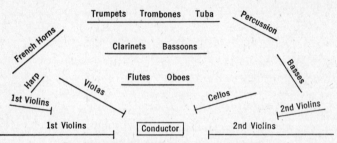

The New England Conservatory Orchestra

the percussion close to the brasses. Care should be taken to see that neither the horns nor the percussion are too close to the back or side walls of the stage. This is the only way to avoid distortion of tone in the case of the horns and overprojection in the case of the percussion.

Before we leave this discussion of physical arrangements on the stage, a word or two is in order about the conductor's podium and music stand. It is most important from the point of view of sight lines between the conductor and his players that the podium should not be too high or too low. It must bear a direct relationship to the height of the conductor, for if it raises his beat and eyes too high, the players immediately around him will not be able to follow his directions without losing all contact with the printed page; if too low, those in the rear and on the far sides will not be able to follow him at all. If the orchestra is to be seated on risers, this must be considered in constructing the podium.

Finally, the conductor's stand must be high enough to enable him to transfer his eyes from the players to the printed page with a minimum of physical effort and without losing complete command of the orchestra in the process; yet it must not be too high, lest it obscure the pattern of the beat or cause embarrassing collisions of the baton with it or with the score.

III

PROGRAM BUILDING

THE careful selection of program material for an amateur orchestra is of the utmost importance, for the success or failure of an entire season may well hinge on the judgment and discretion exercised by the conductor in choosing the works to be performed. The primary considerations, apart from good taste and program balance, must be the technical ability of the orchestra, the available instrumentation (and its strengths and weaknesses), and the amount of rehearsal time at the conductor's disposal.

A good amateur orchestra has two unique assets upon which the conductor can capitalize; these are a natural and easily stimulated enthusiasm for good music and a willingness to tackle any musical problem set before it. If the works selected for the repertory are of high musical standards, and if the technical problems contained therein are not too far beyond its ability, the orchestra will be encouraged by the progress it makes in rehearsal and by the success it achieves in concert. If the music chosen is too consistently difficult, the result can only be discouragement and a feeling of failure—with a consequent undermining of group morale.

To begin with, the program should be a graded one containing music from each of three categories: difficult, moderately difficult, and easy. The proportion of each will be determined entirely by the technical factors listed in the first paragraph above. One major work (or at most two) may present technical and aesthetic problems slightly over the collective heads of the players. These should be just difficult enough to enable them to benefit from working out the solutions, but not so difficult that the work cannot be brought to successful performance at the conclusion of the allotted number of rehearsals. The supporting program should be divided between pieces that will be easy to prepare and those that present problems of moderate difficulty. One of these may be utilized as the opening number of the concert for the dual purpose of "playing the orchestra in" and of allowing the players to conquer the inevitable initial nervousness without undue mental or physical strain.

In considering the instrumentation of his orchestra, the conductor can follow one of two courses: (1) choose or adapt music for the particular combination of instruments at his disposal; (2) ignore its deficiencies and program the Beethoven Fifth Symphony or the Schubert "Unfinished," supplying the missing parts by bringing in a last minute cadre of professionals or by relying on the ubiquitous piano. Needless to say, I feel that it is far better to fit the music to the orchestra. Chapter XI will describe in detail sources of material for orchestras whose instrumentation is incomplete, as well as material that will lend itself to limitless adaptation to meet special requirements. In cases where such a policy, exclusively pursued, unduly limits the musical fare of the orchestra, the conductor should beg or borrow the services of other *amateur* players, not professionals, on the missing instruments. Any other procedure is a negation of the amateur ideal and places the orchestra in a musical demimonde. Credit should be given to these guests on the program.

There is probably not a single conductor of an amateur orchestra who feels that he has at his disposal as much rehearsal time as he needs. Time is, therefore, a major factor in determining the content of the concert program. With one drawn up along the lines previously suggested, it is not difficult to place the rehearsal emphasis on the major work or works and still allot sufficient time to the preparation of the balance of the program. If the conductor errs and chooses a program that is too consistently difficult, the rehearsals will necessarily develop increasingly into high-pressure affairs. The preparation of some of the works will have to be slighted, often at the last moment, and the conductor will be forced to ask for additional rehearsals just before the concert. No amateur group can thrive under these conditions.

In addition to the relative difficulty of each of the works chosen, the actual playing time of the entire program must be kept in mind. As will be pointed out more fully later, it is better to plan a program of moderate proportions, for the sake of both the audience and the orchestra, and thus assure its adequate preparation in a sequence of unhurried, well-planned rehearsals. Unless carefully timed, a program can easily go to one extreme or the other and become either too long or too short. I shall never forget being the co-author of a program performed by the Harvard Orchestra in the college chapel which, though it looked ample on paper, was over in just twenty-nine minutes. As it closed, latecomers were still arriving!

The third consideration in program planning is contrast and/or unity. The more common type of program is one which includes works from different periods, styles, and composers. It achieves variety and interest through combining music from the classic, romantic, impressionist and modern schools; by contrasting full orchestra with small orchestra; or by including works for strings alone or winds alone. It may feature a solo instrument with orchestral accompaniment or a work for chorus and orchestra.

Unity of program may be achieved by limiting it to the works of one composer, of one national school, or of a single period of music history. In general, the first of these should be avoided. A meal consisting solely of five kinds of lamb, no matter how differently each is prepared, would prove uninteresting to both the cook and the consumer. A more satisfactory program for an amateur group can be fashioned from the works of two composers (Bach and Handel, or Bach and Mozart, for example). The program from one national school does not need elaboration here as the content is self-evident. There are many possibilities when one plans an historical program: the sixteenth and seventeenth centuries produced a wealth of orchestral music by such composers as Gabrieli, Corelli, Vivaldi, Scarlatti, Dowland, Morley, Purcell, Bach, and Handel. There are the symphonists of the Mannheim School; Haydn, Mozart, early Beethoven, and so on.

The following are some sample programs, briefly analyzed along the lines discussed so far in this chapter, together with a statement of the conditions under which they were prepared for concert performance.

Contrasting Styles and Periods
PROGRAM A

1. Beethoven: Overture to "Prometheus"
2. Handel: Concerto Grosso in F for strings and continuo
3. Mozart: Symphony No. 35 ("Haffner")

4. Purcell: Andante in F-sharp minor for strings
5. Robert McBride: Fugato on a Well-known Theme

This program was prepared by the Wellesley College Orchestra in about eight weeks, two rehearsals per week of one hour and twenty minutes each. Instrumentation was complete except for the horns called for in numbers 3 and 5, and the trombones in the latter. These instrumentalists were "borrowed" from the Harvard Orchestra for the final rehearsals and the concert. Numbers 1, 3, and 5 are for full orchestra; numbers 2 and 4, for strings alone, with the addition of cembalo (piano) in number 2. All these works have been published except number 4, which was reproduced from manuscript photographs made by the conductor in the British Museum. Numbers 3 and 5 are the difficult pieces; numbers 1 and 2, of moderate difficulty; and number 4 presents no technical problems at all. The Beethoven work answers the requirements for a good opening number.

PROGRAM B

1. Cimarosa: Overture to "Il Matrimonio segreto"
2. Bach: Concerto in D minor for two violins
3. Buxtehude: Chaconne in E minor
4. Grieg: Two lyric pieces for strings
5. Haydn: Symphony in E flat ("Drum Roll")

Program B was prepared by the Harvard University Orchestra in approximately six weeks, two rehearsals per week of two hours each. Instrumentation was complete. Numbers 3 and 5 are the difficult works; numbers 1 and 2, moderately difficult; number 4, comparatively easy. The orchestra that semester included an unusually large number of newcomers, and the difficulty of the program was modified somewhat. All works are pub-

lished except the Buxtehude, which was arranged by
the conductor from an organ work.

With Soloist

PROGRAM C

1. Sir Henry Bishop: Overture to "Love in a Tub"
2. Hindemith: Five Pieces for Strings
3. Mozart: Concerto in A major for Clarinet
4. Hindemith: Trauermusik for solo viola and
   strings
5. Holst: "Brook Green" Suite

This program was prepared by the Wellesley College
Orchestra, with conditions as for program A. The full
orchestra works are numbers 1, 3, and 5. The difficult
numbers are 2 and 3; numbers 4 and 1 are of moderate
difficulty; number 5 is easy. All are published except
number 1, which is from a British Museum manuscript.
A student soloist played the concerto. The orchestra was
privileged to have Mr. Hindemith as guest conductor for
number 2 and as viola soloist in number 4.

PROGRAM D

1. Mozart: Overture to "The Magic Flute"
2. Haydn: Symphony in D major ("Clock")
3. G. Gabrieli: Sonata pian e forte, for brass instruments
4. Mozart: Concerto in A major for piano
5. Bartok: Rumanian Dances

The Harvard University Orchestra prepared this program, with conditions as for program B. This program
has a more consistently high level of difficulty because
the players at that time were largely upperclassmen with
considerable experience. The brass section was unusually

good, and was featured in the Gabrieli sonata. The soloist in the Mozart was a member of the Harvard Music Department.

PROGRAM E

1. Handel: Concerto for Grand Orchestra
2. Fauré: Prelude from the "Pelleas and Melisande" Suite
3. A. Scarlatti: Fugue from the Suite for Flute and Strings
4. Beethoven: Concerto in C major for Piano (first movement)
5. Barber: Adagio for Strings
6. Haydn: Symphony in B flat Major (No. 8 of the London set)

This program was prepared by the Orchestra of the Greenwood Music Camp consisting of young people from eleven to eighteen years of age plus four faculty members, in six weeks of rehearsals, twice a week for one hour and forty-five minutes. Instrumentation was complete except for second bassoon and second horn. Numbers 5 and 6, difficult; numbers 2 and 4, moderately difficult; numbers 1 and 3 easy. The soloist was an eleven-year-old camper.

Program Featuring Two Composers
PROGRAM F

1. Handel: Concerto Grosso (B & H No. 24) for strings and wind
2. Bach: Sonatina from Cantata 182, "God's Time Is Best"
3. Bach: Concerto in F minor for klavier and strings
4. Bach: Brandenburg Concerto No. 5 in D major
5. Handel: Sinfonia to "Ottone"

This program is well suited for orchestras with limited instrumentation. Numbers 1 and 5 both call for strings and a few winds, and may be expanded by means of careful editing to include other instruments which are available but not scored in the original version. Number 2 calls for two flutes, violas, cellos, and basses; number 4, for a solo violin, flute, and piano accompanied by strings. Number 5 was arranged for full orchestra by the conductor. The music of this particular period has another advantage for the small amateur orchestra in that the conventional *continuo* part gives the conductor an opportunity to use available piano talent.

The Historical Program

The following two programs are examples of what may be done in presenting music illustrating a particular historical sequence. They are the first two of a series of three concerts given by the Wellesley College Orchestra in 1934–35 illustrating the development of instrumental music from 1492 to Mozart. They were planned primarily to supplement college courses in music history and appreciation, but complete texts and extensive program notes made it possible for the general public to understand and enjoy the various works. Several examples of choral music were included as a matter of interest and for purposes of contrast.

PROGRAM G

1. Purcell: Dance Suite for Flute and Strings
2. Madrigal Group:
     Canon: "Hey, ho to the Greenwood," Byrd
     Madrigal: "The Silver Swan," Gibbons
     Round: "Old Bridge's Epitaph," Anon. Ms.
3. G. Gabrieli: Two canzoni per sonar a quattro

4. Pezel: Tower Music for Brass Instruments
5. Anon.: Sinfonia (Fifteenth Century)
6. Dowland: Lachrimae Antiquae for Divers Instruments and Voyces
7. Palestrina: Ricercare del sesto tono
8. Tower Chorales for Brass: Kugelman
   Anon. (Mainz, 1514)
9. A. Scarlatti: Sinfonia to "La Rosaura"

A program of this sort calls for considerable research on the part of the conductor in unearthing historical material and editing it for his particular instrumentation. With the exception of number 2, there is not a single number listed that is not adaptable for any combination of instruments under the sun, from four recorders to a full symphony orchestra. Such a program has a special value for schools and colleges, as it affords music students and others the opportunity to hear actual performances of music which they might otherwise only see printed in textbooks and anthologies. Very little of this type of early instrumental music has been recorded. Program G covers the period from 1492 to 1694, and the following programs (one of which is given—program H) carry on from 1600, a slight retrogression, to Mozart.

PROGRAM H

1. Rosenmuller: Studentenmusik Suite in C major
2. Bach: Concerto in D minor for two violins
3. Henry VIII of England: Two Instrumental Pieces for Viols
4. Bach: Cantata No. 202: "Weichet nur, betrübte Schatten" for Soprano, Oboe, Strings, and Organ
5. Gretry: Overture to "Le Ríval Confident"

Numbers 1 and 2 are published; numbers 4 and 5 are available in score in the complete works of these two composers; number 3 was arranged for strings by the conductor from photographs of a British Museum manuscript.

The Orchestra of Limited Instrumentation

PROGRAM I

1. Rosenmuller: Studentenmusik Suite in D minor
2. Warlock: Capriol Suite
3. Haydn: Andante from the "Surprise" symphony
4. Bach: Concerto in C major for three Klavier and Strings
5. Gluck: Suite from the ballet-pantomime "Don Juan"

This program was prepared by the Radcliffe College Orchestra, at that time consisting of a complete string section, three flutes, two clarinets, one horn, two trumpets, tympani, and piano. All these works except number 5 are published. The latter is available in full score in the Denkmaler Tonkunst series. The original instrumentation of numbers 1, 2, and 5 was either added to or adapted for the needs of the orchestra in question.

PROGRAM J

1. Purcell-Holst: Suite from "The Virtuous Wife"
2. Handel: Concerto Grosso in F major for Strings and Cembalo
3. J. C. Bach: Sinfonia in B flat Major
4. Vaughan-Williams: Variants on "Dives and Lazarus" for Strings and Harp (Piano)
5. Bach-Vaughan-Williams: "Giant" Fugue in G minor

This program was designed for the student orchestra of the Greenwood Music Camp the year before program E. The instrumentation then was complete strings, four flutes, one oboe, three clarinets, one bassoon, and piano. All these works are published. Only number 5 had to be adapted for the orchestra by the addition of wind and brass parts (the original called for strings only).

Additional program material will be found in the appendix, and a further discussion of sources of program material in Chapter XI.

To sum up program making for the amateur orchestra: (1) The music chosen should be of uncompromisingly high standards, for the sake of the players and of the audience as well. (2) The programs should serve a double purpose: to bring the player and the listener into contact with representative works from the standard orchestral literature, *provided* the orchestra is technically able to cope successfully with those works; and to explore the vast quantity of literature now lying fallow outside the well-worked field of the professional orchestra. (3) A most careful proportion should be worked out between pieces that are difficult to prepare and pieces that are not, with the technical ability of the orchestra, its instrumentation, and the amount of pre-concert rehearsal time at its disposal constantly in mind.

IV

REHEARSAL PLANNING

PREPARING an amateur orchestra for a concert is always a race against time. The conductor has to face the inexorable fact that he has but a limited number of rehearsals at his disposal and a fairly inflexible amount of time per rehearsal. He cannot afford, therefore, to limit his planning to improvising work schedules from one rehearsal to the next. Concerts have an insidious habit of creeping up surreptitiously on the conductor who follows this procedure.

To take the utmost advantage of the available rehearsal time, the conductor should draw up in advance two plans of attack: first, an over-all plan which takes into account the total number of rehearsals and the general objectives which must be attained during their course; second, a detailed plan of the individual rehearsals based on a minute analysis of the technical difficulties contained in the music itself.

The over-all plan may be divided into three phases with three separate objectives: (1) to become acquainted in a general way with each of the pieces on the program; (2) to work intensively on solving the various technical and musical problems contained therein; (3) to recreate the beauty, mood, and inner meaning of each. These three processes must be dealt with separately in working with amateurs, for they cannot be carried on simultaneously with success.

Isolation of technical problems is the keynote of the detailed plan. The players must be brought face to face with the most difficult passages on the program for the purpose of concentrating on mastering them to the exclusion of all else. This procedure calls for a time schedule for each individual rehearsal drawn up as rehearsals progress but within the framework of the over-all plan devised before the season begins.

The over-all plan just mentioned divides the total number of rehearsals into three categories—reading rehearsals, detailed rehearsals, and final rehearsals. The proportion of each might be as follows: reading rehearsals, a little less than one-fifth of the total; detailed rehearsals, three-fifths; final rehearsals, the remainder. Thus a college orchestra producing one concert per semester in twenty rehearsals would have three reading, twelve detailed, and five final rehearsals.

The function of each of these three categories may be defined as follows:

Reading Rehearsals: To read through each work on the program in its entirety, if possible without stopping, in order to give the players a bird's-eye view—a look at the entire landscape, if you will, before settling down to the study of individual bits of the topography. These rehearsals serve a three-fold purpose: (1) They help to arouse the interest and enthusiasm of the players in the program. (2) They provide the conductor with valuable information regarding the strengths and weaknesses of the orchestra in relation to the music he has chosen. (3) They afford practice in the art of sight reading.

Detailed Rehearsals: To isolate all the passages presenting problems of technique, intonation, rhythm, or ensemble, and to concentrate on mastering them, to the exclusion of the simpler passages.

Final Rehearsals: To resume the study of each work as a whole and to concentrate on interpretation for the purpose of bringing to life the beauty latent in the music.

The reasons for the reading rehearsals have been stated and are, it seems to me, self-evident. A word of explanation is needed, however, about the purpose of dividing the remaining rehearsal time between work on details and on what may be termed the recreative process. Through practical experience and observation, I have come to believe strongly that the best concert results are obtained only by having the orchestra concentrate on one problem at a time, each problem reduced to its simplest terms. Amateur players cannot be expected to learn the notes, solve the rhythmic problems, observe the phrase markings and the dynamic indications, and follow the conductor's beat all at the same time. When this is attempted, progress is slow and unsatisfactory to the conductor and the players alike. Much of the work of one rehearsal has to be reviewed at the next, for the mind cannot be expected to assimilate, nor the memory to retain, details of instruction under so many and such varied headings.

First things must come first. In the detailed rehearsals, therefore, the orchestra concentrates on the problems which have been isolated for them by the conductor. The rehearsal time is spent entirely on the passages containing these problems. No attempt is made to distract the players from their preoccupation with notes and rhythms by insisting on more than a superficial adherence to the indicated dynamics. The conductor chooses a rehearsal tempo that is conservative compared to the eventual concert tempo. As the orchestra makes progress in solving the technical problems, the tempo is gradually increased. Except for attacks, releases, and holds, the players are not necessarily required to pay close attention to the conductor's beat during these rehearsals.

The success of the final rehearsals and the concert will depend entirely on the efficiency and thoroughness with which the technical and rhythmic foundations are laid in these rehearsals on details. Only a thorough knowledge of the notes can free the players from the printed page. Then, and then only, can the conductor have the degree of control over his forces that is so vitally necessary when the orchestra comes to grips with the problems of interpretation in the final rehearsals. Here, and in the concert, he must be able to demand and obtain a quick and unanimous response to his gestures.

The following will show how the reading rehearsal plan is applied to a specific program. The following works were prepared by the Wellesley College Orchestra in nineteen rehearsals of one hour and twenty minutes each. Of these nineteen rehearsals, three were devoted to reading through the various numbers.

1. Hadyn: Overture to "L'Isola disabitata"
2. Vivaldi: Concerto in G minor for Strings and Cembalo
3. Mozart: Symphonie Concertante in E flat, for violin and viola
4. Vaughan-Williams: Fantasy on a theme of Thomas Tallis for double string orchestra
5. Ballantine: Variations on "Mary Had a Little Lamb"

All are published except number 5. Numbers 3 and 4 are difficult; numbers 1 and 5, moderately difficult; number 2 is easy.

Each of the pieces was timed in advance, movement

by movement, and a time schedule drawn up for the individual rehearsals. In this way, the conductor was assured that the required ground could be covered in the allotted number of rehearsals. The results were as follows:

READING REHEARSALS

Rehearsal 1

　　Haydn Overture (complete)

　　Ballantine: Theme and first three variations

　　Mozart: First movement (without soloists)

　　Vivaldi: First movement

Rehearsal 2

　　Ballantine: Completion

　　Mozart: Second movement (without soloists)

　　Vivaldi: Second movement

　　Vaughan-Williams: 1st half

Rehearsal 3

　　Mozart: Third movement (without soloists)

　　Vivaldi: Third movement

　　Vaughan-Williams: 2nd half

A departure from the stated plan of sight reading the entire program had to be made in the case of the Vaughan-Williams Fantasy. Because of its technical difficulty and the complex way in which the string section has to be divided, it was assigned for individual outside practice before rehearsal. Both halves of the work, therefore, were prepared rather than read at sight.

The only actual training the orchestra receives during the reading rehearsals, apart from attacks, releases, and holds, is in the vital matter of individual and sectional tuning. This cannot be stressed too early nor too often, for it is the sole foundation upon which a successful amateur orchestra can be built. Many such orchestras can, and do, play extraordinarily well, only to have their fine work nullified by inaccurate or slipshod tuning. Such a parlous state of affairs is inexcusable, and the blame can be laid at but one door—the conductor's. No rehearsal should be begun until the entire orchestra has been tuned carefully, not in a wild melee of fortissimo A's. Unless ruthlessly drilled, the players will begin to tune even before the correct pitch has been sounded, mingling the hurly-burly with snatches of the Mendelssohn violin concerto, "Til Eulenspiegal," and "Lenore No. 3." In the early stages of tuning discipline, it may even be necessary to tune by individuals, but quiet tuning by sections should be the primary objective. However, this is only the beginning, for the pitch must be checked before every number on the rehearsal schedule. In addition, the word "intonation" should be brought up every quarter-hour, on the quarter-hour—oftener if the occasion calls for it, and it will. Tuning discipline in rehearsal must be so stringent and so well organized that by the time of the first public concert the orchestra will be capable of adjusting accurately, quickly, and quietly to the given pitch with a minimum of extraneous music-making.

There remains to be discussed the question of marking uniform bowings, fingerings, and phrasing in the parts. With orchestras of elementary school age, this has to be done entirely by the conductor. With high-school, college, and community orchestras, there is much to be gained from having the principals of the various sections take over this responsibility. The conductor may or may not need to serve as advisor. If he does, a series of meetings with the principals may be held as the reading rehearsals progress and while the music is fresh in their minds. The conductor should allow the players the freest possible expression of their ideas, advising as much as possible, but making the final decisions himself. If he overrules a suggestion from a player, he should take care to give his reasons. This coöperative system enables the players to obtain valuable experience under expert guidance, and also makes them feel that they are an integral part of the organization of the orchestra.

This work is important because its objectives are to secure uniform bowing in each string section, to give fingerings which may facilitate the playing of difficult passages, to secure uniform phrasing in the winds and brasses, and to check the work of the editor. Under this last division I would include making changes where the editing is impractical for the particular orchestra in question, or where the editing is in questionable musical taste. (See practically any orchestral edition of the works of Bach or Handel.) With the completion of this task, the work of the reading rehearsals is over.

V

DETAILED REHEARSALS

BY the time the reading rehearsals are completed, the conductor will have in his possession the fullest information about the potentialities of every section of the orchestra. He will also know what passages in each of the works on the program are going to prove the most difficult from the point of view of technique, intonation, rhythm, or balance. It is on these passages, and these alone, that the orchestra will concentrate during the detailed rehearsals.

The conductor must analyze the results of the reading rehearsals with the greatest care. The most difficult passages will need to be assigned for individual outside practice and, in addition, receive the greatest amount of rehearsal time. Those of medium difficulty may require separate rehearsing on the part of a particular section or even an individual player (wind or brass), while passages of negligible technical difficulty but involving problems of balance between sections may be worked out in regular rehearsals.

The analysis of the program cited in the preceding chapter was as follows:

Haydn: Main theme of the allegro section difficult for the cellos and basses; moderately difficult for the violins and violas. An ensemble problem involving correct balance among the strings, once the running passages are mastered. Outside practice for the horns in transposition and at least one brass and wind section rehearsal with the conductor.

Vivaldi: Very little need for detailed work in rehearsal. Some passages for individual private practice. An early start may be made on "playing the piece in." By this is meant becoming thoroughly acquainted with the work by playing it through, stopping only occasionally when the need arises. The players may come to grips with problems of balance and interpretation almost at once without waiting for the final rehearsals.

Mozart: Many difficult passages for all sections, about equally divided between the first and last movements. Because of the form of these movements, with constant thematic repetition in the original or related keys, the technical mastery of one passage usually means the mastery of several others—except, of course, for any intonation problems which may arise through modulation. Rehearsal time may be concentrated on the orchestral *tuttis,* for the accompaniments to solo passages are invariably simple. The main problem in the latter will be to achieve balance between the solo instruments and the orchestra. A beginning on this will be made toward the end of the detailed rehearsals, when the soloists will make their first appearance.

Vaughan-Williams: The technical problems of the individual sections lie mostly in passages in the higher positions for the violins and cellos. These must be assigned for outside practice, along with the passages for solo string quartet. The quartet must also be coached by the conductor outside of the regular rehearsals. There is one difficult passage for the entire string orchestra which poses both technical and rhythmic problems. (See the example at the end of this chapter.) Apart from this, the main problem is that of balance between the two orchestras and the solo quartet. The conductor must take great pains to divide the string talent at his disposal evenly between the two orchestras.

Ballantine: These brief and humorous variations in the styles of various composers are not technically difficult except for those in imitation of Wagner and Debussy. Of all the numbers on the program, only these two variations and the Haydn overture seem to call for wind and brass sectional rehearsals. One-half hour of concentrated work on each will probably suffice.

At the last reading rehearsal, the conductor announces the exact schedule for the first of the detailed rehearsals and makes specific assignments of passages for individual outside practice. If the morale and group spirit of the orchestra is already high, it will not be necessary to dwell on the importance of individual coöperation in this matter. If the conductor is in the process of creating or developing these indispensable elements, it will be well to point out that time is short and that the progress of the orchestra will be retarded if time has to be taken in rehearsal to allow procrastinators to do their practicing in public. As a general rule, it is not a good policy to require any member of an amateur orchestra to play alone for purposes other than constructive criticism. I would make an exception to this rule in the case of those isolated individuals who prove to be non-coöperative or lax in outside practice. Such a procedure will encourage the workers and stimulate the drones, for it will show that the conductor is in earnest. The orchestra is better off without the services of players who do not respond to such an obvious hint.

It takes a great deal of effort and careful thought to plan individual time schedules for a whole sequence of detailed rehearsals, but the results more than justify the painstaking care entailed. Without a schedule as a guide, it is fatally easy for the conductor to become absorbed in one particular problem and devote a disproportionate amount of time to it, to the ultimate detriment of the over-all preparation of the program. This, in turn, deprives the orchestra of the variety it should find in the work of each rehearsal and undermines the players' interest.

The advantages of the time schedule are these: (1) It helps the conductor to turn every single minute of the rehearsal to good account, and prevents needless waste of time. (2) It is the means by which rehearsal emphasis may be proportioned evenly among *all* the difficult passages in such a way that none is slighted and all are adequately prepared. (3) It tells the players in advance what to prepare for each rehearsal. (4) Its self-evident efficiency builds morale, not only by example but by such a simple courtesy as telling each player when his services will be needed and when they will not. One note of warning about rehearsal schedules: I know from experience that the conductor will have to use considerable self-discipline in the matter of adhering to the time schedule once he has drawn it up, lest he destroy its effectiveness.

To illustrate the use of schedules with the program under discussion:

Rehearsal 4

4:40–4:55. Haydn Overture: A warm-up run through the entire work (6 minutes); detailed passage-work in the introduction and the first allegro at a reduced tempo (9 minutes).

4:55–5:25. Mozart: First movement: entire time on details of a few passages, working with strings alone, winds alone, then the entire orchestra together. Some work with an individual string section if required.

5:25–5:30. Brief pause for announcements, and setting the stage for the next number. Winds, brass, and percussion excused.

5:30–5:50. Vaughan-Williams: Opening section to letter D, working on rhythm, intonation, and technique. Some work by sections in the difficult spots. Rehearsal ends with a nonstop playing of the assignment to D to consolidate the gains thus far made.

Rehearsal 5

4:40–5:00. Ballantine: The two variations in the styles of Tschaikovsky and Wagner; the former used as a warm-up piece with a little additional detailed work; concentration on passages from the latter.

5:00–5:25. Mozart: Third movement: concentration on the main theme of this Rondo solves two-thirds of the movement.

5:25–5:30. (See Rehearsal 4.)

5:30–5:50. Vaughan-Williams: Review work of the previous rehearsal without stopping; continue work on details to letter E or F (depending on the rate of progress).

One by one, the various orchestral problems presented by each of the works on the program are introduced into the rehearsal schedules for dissection, working out, and review at the end of each of the periods assigned. If not more than two schedules are posted at a time, the emphasis may easily be kept in a constant state of flux and shifted from one problem to another as the need develops. Care must be taken to see that there is not too long a lapse of time between successive appearances of a given passage or movement in rehearsal lest the gains cease to be cumulative.

There are several ways in which necessary sectional rehearsals may be incorporated into this plan. The conductor will seldom feel able to devote an entire rehearsal to one section unless he has an assistant and can hold two concurrent rehearsals. If he has not, one solution would be to devote the end of a rehearsal to one particular section, excusing the other players (see Rehearsals 4 and 5). A corollary to this would be to begin a rehearsal with one section and have the full orchestra report at a predetermined later time. This allows both the conductor and the players a higher degree of concentration than is possible at a rehearsal of the full orchestra and avoids the loss of interest which invariably results when too much sectional work is attempted with all the players present.

In the detailed rehearsals, the conductor must constantly strive to isolate a technical problem, reduce it to its simplest terms, and show the players specifically how to solve it. In this connection, one concrete and well-chosen example is worth a hundred words of explanation. Conductors, as a class, are a wordy lot. I have actually seen, perhaps I should say heard, a young man spend twenty minutes on the first sixteen bars of a Handel overture. The time was divided as follows: four minutes of playing; a twelve-minute lecture on Handel's melodic line and a short history of the violin bow from the sixteenth century to Tourte; four minutes of repetition of the same sixteen bars. Needless to say, the repetition contained the same faults that the conductor had correctly noted in the first place.

The amateur player wants to be told just two things about his mistakes—what is wrong and how to correct it.

The best way to answer these two questions is for the conductor to borrow an instrument and do his own demonstrating; the second best is to call upon a key player to do this for him. In many cases, the point may be made even more quickly by singing. The conductor should not be deterred from resorting to vocal illustrations even if his singing verges on public scandal. If, as a last resort, words must be used to solve a technical impasse, let the explanation be mercifully brief.

One of the basic problems that must be faced in these detailed rehearsals is the matter of orchestral balance. In nine cases out of ten, the dynamics indicated in the score and the parts are misleading. For example, in a given passage all the voices may be uniformly marked fortissimo. If the players are allowed to interpret this literally, the main theme and any important counterpoint may easily be covered by the purely harmonic material given to other instruments—the brasses, for example. This is particularly true when the main theme is in an inner voice. A given passage must be taken apart in order that the players may see exactly how it is constructed, and how the melody, counterpoint, and harmony are distributed among the several instruments. Only then can they successfully be taught to subordinate themselves and to play slightly *below* the indicated dynamic when they do not have the main theme or important contrapuntal material. A constant give-and-take between sections is the only basis for satisfactory balance in orchestral playing.

Although the isolation of technical difficulties is of assistance in rehearsal, many problems need, in addition, to be reduced to their simplest terms. For example, a passage involving the use of trills, appoggiaturas, or other ornaments should first be practiced without them. The rhythm of a passage containing these devices is usually pulled off center when the players try to cope with everything at once. The passage should first be mastered in its simplest form and then, with the basic rhythm firmly established, the ornaments can be added.

Concentrated drill of this sort is invaluable in developing cohesion and unity within a section, as well as balance between sections. The conductor must not accept less than the players' best efforts in working on details, and must not leave a given problem until the predetermined amount of progress for that particular rehearsal has been attained. No matter how great the concentration may be at a given moment, the conductor cannot afford to let errors of pitch, note value, or rhythm pass unchecked.

Careful attention must be paid to indications which underline or displace the normal accent of the measure, such as >, *fp, sfz,* and *rinf.* The difficulty will be to teach the players the correct interpretation of each of these effects and to secure the universal participation in them of *all* the players. It is not enough for a few players to respond. Too often such rhythmic variations as these, which add spice and drive to the interpretation, are so weak that they are audible only on the stage. If anything, they must be overdone if the composer's full intent is to be conveyed to the audience.

Syncopation is another amateur stumbling block. The difficulty the conductor has to face is in obtaining the clean articulation of each syncopated beat so necessary for the successful execution of this type of rhythm. The common faults are too legato an approach in bowing and tonguing, which muddies the rhythm and gives the passage a languid, inanimate sound out of keeping with the composer's intent; or an involuntary crescendo on each off-beat which gives a monotonous seesaw effect, thus:

On the contrary, each beat in a syncopated passage should be cleanly and articulated if the rhythmic push and pull between the on-beats and the off-beats is to be effectively conveyed to the listener, thus:

The only exception to this rule would be in a passage such as that in the first movement of the Mozart D minor concerto for piano, where a legato syncopation is obviously indicated:

Inexperienced players seem to have difficulty in playing a triplet rhythm accurately. For example, a figure such as

They also find a figure like the following completely bewildering.

Much painstaking drill, preceded by a careful demonstration on the part of the conductor, will be needed to master these and the more intricate rhythmic patterns. A useful device for rhythmic practice is to have the players go over a particular passage without their instruments, tapping out the rhythm on the music stand or merely clapping their hands. This reduces the problem to its essentials by removing, for the time being, the technical and pitch complications. A few extra minutes of this sort of practice will save rehearsal time by fixing the correct rhythmic pattern firmly in the minds of the players before they are asked to play it on their instruments.

There is one important physiological element to be considered in drawing up rehearsal time schedules: fatigue among the players. It is well to begin the rehearsal with a comparatively easy number, to allow the players to limber up; but this should be followed by the most difficult work on the schedule, while the orchestra is still fresh. The greatest progress will be made during the early and middle stages of a rehearsal, before the players begin to tire and their powers of concentration to weaken. The technical demands upon the orchestra should, whenever possible, taper off toward the end, but in any event the conductor should endeavor to lighten the intensity of the work as the rehearsal progresses.

Another way to keep rehearsal efficiency at a high level and at the same time introduce the element of variety is to allot a short period in one or two of the detailed rehearsals to sight reading. This device postpones the onset of physical and mental fatigue in the individual rehearsal, and also gives the players a momentary respite from the necessarily hard work of preparing for the concert.

From Vaughan Williams, *Fantasia on a Theme by Thomas Tallis for Double Stringed Orchestra* (Copyright, 1921, by Goodwin and Tabb, Ltd.). Reproduced by permission of G. Schirmer, Inc., New York, and J. Curwen and Sons Ltd., London.

VI

FINAL REHEARSALS

Up to this point in the development of the concert program, the conductor has functioned chiefly as a teacher and musical disciplinarian. His two objectives have been to show the players how to master the music under preparation; to mold individuals into well-integrated sections, and those sections into a cohesive, vertebrate whole. In so doing, he has been laying the foundation for his ultimate goal: to re-create in sound the beauty he finds in the scores. The acid test of the conductor as a teacher will be the degree of success he attains as a creative artist with his amateur group.

The re-creative process calls for sound musicianship, sensitive emotion, and—above all—imagination. The conductor needs to have a complete command of the scores in order to plan the performance of each, detail by detail. He must be able to obtain the utmost contrast between movements, and even between themes, without sacrificing the necessary continuity and flow of musical thought. He must temper the re-creative process to the period and style of the individual composer if he is to avoid producing a program completely in the image of his own artistic ego. Mozart must not sound like Schubert, Beethoven like Brahms, nor Tschaikovsky like a storm in a cavern. This is not the elementary cliché it may seem, for the prevalent frenetic approach to conducting which dominates our concert halls today invariably reduces the various composers to their lowest common denominator—the conductor. Artistic integrity demands that the performance of each work be as close to the composer's indicated intent as the conductor's musicianship and the ability of his players will allow.

A mastery of the score, however, is not enough. The final and indispensable elements are emotional sensitivity and imagination, for these determine whether the music really lives in sound or merely exists. The conductor must not only feel deeply the emotional content of the music but must be able to teach his players to feel it as well, if the performance is to have warmth, sincerity, and depth with which to convince the hearer. Inner conviction, communicated to amateur musicians through the medium of inspirational leadership, can easily cause them to rise above their technical limitations.

In order to achieve success in the re-creative process, the conductor must have the orchestra, figuratively speaking, in the palm of his hand. He has prepared the way for this in the detailed rehearsals by seeing to it that the players learn the notes of the most difficult passages thoroughly. The first concern of the final rehearsals must be to pry the players loose from their preoccupation with the music itself. The word "pry" is used advisedly here, for the printed page exercises an almost hypnotic power over the amateur player. If left to his own devices, he will see the initial beat and the final release but not much in between.

One way of overcoming this habit and, at the same time, of achieving increased control over the entire orchestra is to take a given passage and require the players to follow the conductor in a number of capricious and purely arbitrary deviations from the normal interpretation. This game of musical follow-the-leader quickly becomes a battle of wits which accomplishes the desired results with a minimum of drudgery and a maximum of amusement for all concerned. There is an infinite number of variations of tempo and dynamics which may be employed: for example, holds prolonged beyond their normal length; delayed final chords, a most effective device, as those who are not watching closely will come in all by themselves; a previously rehearsed ritard may be eliminated, or one inserted at an unexpected spot; one section may suddenly be called on to subdue itself while another is brought forward. This procedure will quickly train the players to look up frequently without losing their places in the music, and will speed up their instinctive responses to the indications of the conductor's baton and left hand, not to mention his eyes and facial expression. To reinforce this sort of training, the conductor should give many cues for entrances of important thematic material and teach his players to watch for them. The high degree of control which will result from practice of this sort will enable the conductor to capitalize on the emotional sensitivity which develops under concert conditions. Given this control over his forces, the conductor can achieve greater freedom of interpretation in concert than has ever been attained in rehearsal. The result will be a performance that is a stimulating emotional and artistic experience for the audience and the players alike.

Naturally, the conductor must have both the craftsmanship and the personality necessary to make a success of this technique. If he has, all he will need to do in the final rehearsals is to indicate the main outlines of the re-creative process as he conceives them, leaving the ulti-

mate achievement of plasticity of line, phrase, and in-
condescent inner beauty for the concert itself. I realize
that this seems like a dangerous procedure to attempt
with amateurs, but I have seen it succeed many times.
It will succeed, however, only when the players have been
so well coached in rehearsal that they come to the concert
with complete confidence in themselves and their ability
to play the program before them. The only alternative
to this approach is for the conductor to impose his interpretive ideas by rote. This is a formidable task, as in a
given program there will be a thousand and one small
details to be worked out and remembered. There is never
enough rehearsal time to make this feasible. Even if there
were, the collective memory of amateur players would not
be able to retain so much material.

To indicate what is meant by "the main outlines of the
re-creative process," I would like to turn specifically to
the work of the final rehearsals and discuss it under the
following headings: tempo and rhythm, nuance, and
emotion.

Tempo and Rhythm

All the rehearsals in the final period must be con-
ducted at the tempi the conductor intends to use in the
concert, in order to fix them firmly in the minds of the
players. The various artificial devices the conductor may
have used during the detailed rehearsals for keeping the
orchestra together, such as counting aloud, tapping the
baton on the stand, or even stamping his foot, must be
abandoned completely. Needless to say, none of these
should be used in the concert, nor should the conductor
indulge in any public singing! Where difficult passages
have previously been taken at a moderate tempo, the

increase to concert speed should be made gradually, rather than all at once, in order that the necessary technical adjustments may be made with a minimum of confusion and loss of rehearsal efficiency.

The orchestra must be taught to establish the correct tempo and the basic rhythm from the very first measure, for one of the outstanding failings of the average amateur orchestra is its tendency to take four or five measures to settle down to what is indicated in the parts. The conductor must see to it that the players have an accurate mental picture of these two elements in order that they may be established from the very start. To assure this, the beginning of every piece or movement must be rehearsed several times at each playing. It is helpful, both in rehearsal and in concert, to give at least two preparatory beats before the orchestra begins to play. As an additional safeguard, the orchestra might well be required to memorize the first one or two measures in order to watch the conductor even more closely during the first few critical moments of a piece. All changes and departures from the initial tempo or rhythm must be quickly observed and immediately conveyed to the ear of the listener. Here again, the amateur needs to be trained to avoid a delayed reaction or a momentary indecision.

The orchestra must also be shown how to differentiate between the strong and weak beats of any given rhythm in order to avoid a feeling of monotony—unless such a feeling is the deliberate intent of the composer. The tendency of the amateur player is to treat each beat of a measure as though it were of equal rhythmic importance. Carefully indicated phrasings and accent in the winds and brasses and bowing in the strings will be a great help in this regard, but it must be supplemented by careful drilling and an explanation of the function of strong and weak beats in the various measure types.

The clipping of note values is an occupational disease with amateur orchestras, to the very great detriment of the mass of orchestral tone, the harmonic background, and the basic rhythm. The conductor will undoubtedly find it necessary to give at least one illustrated lecture per season on the general subject "How Long Is a Quarter-note?" This should show just where in the conducting pattern a quarter-note begins to sound and where it *should* end. It is not difficult to prove, by actual demonstration, that the "mortality rate" among the players increases as the baton approaches the "click" of the second beat until practically no one is giving the quarter-note its full value. Unless note values are carefully observed by *all* the players, the general effect will be destroyed in one of the following ways: (1) The forward flow of the melodic line will be interrupted and the phrase itself cut up into seemingly unrelated bits. (2) The harmonic structure will be weakened by the absence or gradual decrescendo of an important note caused by the premature dropping out of players. (3) The composite orchestral tone will lose strength and depth and will seem constantly to be afflicted by anemia.

The rhythmic and melodic content of each measure must be related to the phrase of which it is a part in order to avoid the sound of a succession of small units lacking in coherence, however accurately played. Amateur orchestras tend to produce phrases which are both metronomic and vertical in their effect upon the listener. The reason for this is too literal an interpretation on the part of the player of the function and intent of the bar-line. At best, the bar-line is an artificial device used for metrical convenience. The players must be shown how an unimaginative adherence to its surface implications results in splitting the phrase into small, incoherent fragments and/or the production of a monotonous, static, melodic line.

For example, if the players are dealing with an eight-measure musical sentence, with perhaps a comma after the fourth measure, they must be taught to keep the phrase in motion throughout its entire length and not convert the comma into a period. The cell-like enclosures between bar-lines may trick the player into subdividing the sentence into small units and so destroy the continuity of musical thought. "Forget the bar-lines and feel the sweep of the phrase" should be the conductor's advice.

Nuance

The principal problem to be faced under this heading is how to widen the effective dynamic range of the orchestra. The normal habitat of the amateur orchestra is somewhere in the vicinity of forte. It has no visible difficulty in rising to an uncontrolled fortissimo and, if sufficiently urged, will now and then subside to a reluctant, and temporary, mezzo-forte. The softer dynamics lie in terra incognita.

The first step is to bring the fortissimo under control and to curb its wild abandon. The worst offenders in this regard are the percussion, brass, and woodwind—in about that order. The players of these instruments seem to hold the theory that the way to produce a stunning fortissimo is to beat or blow their instruments out of shape. Arturo Toscanini is quoted as having said that there is a point beyond which music ceases to be music and becomes mere noise. This homely truth should be posted in every rehearsal and concert hall, amateur and professional alike. The conductor must call a halt every time a fortissimo gets out of hand if he is to eradicate this basic fault.

The second step in widening the dynamic range, the achievement of a true piano and pianissimo, is much more difficult and will require much concentrated drill. Any amateur orchestra can play loudly, but only a well-trained one can play softly. The strings must be taught to exploit fully the different tone qualities which may be obtained between the bridge and the finger board at varying distances from the former. For example, the softer the dynamic, the nearer the bow to the finger board (and conversely). Since there is a universal tendency to play always on the outside edge of the bow-hair, the string players must be made aware of the connection between the dynamic and the amount of bow-hair in contact with the string, and also with the speed with which the bow is drawn. In general, these two elements in tone production for strings vary directly with the dynamic. The function of the vibrato is also not fully understood by the amateur player. He needs to be taught, for example, to employ a narrower and less rapid vibrato in soft passages than he does in loud passages. The winds and brasses must be coached to have as much breath behind the tone in a piano as in a forte, but to control with the greatest care the amount used. The tone produced must be soft, but it must not be characterless or flabby.

This leads directly to another point which must be made in regard to the piano and pianissimo orchestral tone in general: the tone quality at these levels must still have shape and form, an inner core if you will, unless the composer deliberately calls for a *flautato* effect. The conductor ought not to allow his players to produce a soft dynamic by the common process of removing all pressure of the bow on the string and all tension from the air column. Such a tone has neither beauty, depth, nor carrying power. But the battle is only half won when the conductor succeeds in teaching the proper technique for playing softly. He must stop the drill constantly to thwart the letting up of concentration which produces a gradual crescendo where none is indicated, and must be prepared to go over and over soft passages until the physical and mental discipline necessary to produce the desired result has become second nature to the players. It is far more demanding to play piano and pianissimo than it is to play forte and fortissimo.

The sudden piano and sudden forte present another type of problem to the amateur player. Only the most literal interpretation of this effective device will be successful, and yet the tendency is to anticipate it by means of a gradual decrescendo or crescendo, as the case may be, which completely destroys its impact on the ear. The players must be taught to keep the dynamic up (or down) until the last note of the preceding passage has been played, and to establish the new dynamic on the *first* note of the new phrase.

The physical and emotional effectiveness of a crescendo or decrescendo is reduced if the gradual change of dynamic is poorly spaced along the indicated number of measures or beats. The tendency of the amateur orchestra is to make the change too soon and so to reach the zenith (or nadir) of the phrase prematurely. This is particularly apparent where the composer has indicated that the dynamic change is to be made *poco a poco* and has spread the effect over seven, eight, or more measures. The orchestra must be carefully drilled to hold back the development of these two effects and to distribute the change evenly over the entire phrase area to be traversed. The basic patterns:

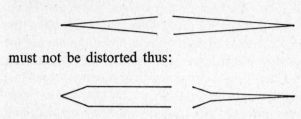

must not be distorted thus:

There is another important element to be considered in obtaining an effective crescendo or decrescendo, and that is the rate of speed with which the various sections should change the dynamic. In a crescendo, for example, the brass and percussion should lag behind the strings and woodwind at first, saving their power for the final few measures and the climax itself. If all the sections progress at the same dynamic rate, the brass and percussion will soon overpower the strings and woodwind and utterly destroy the orchestral balance. Even though this common procedure is guaranteed to bring down the house, it is aesthetically indefensible. Since the score and parts seldom make any differentiation, the conductor will have to exercise sound musical judgment in coaching each section to perform its proper function in the over-all orchestral pattern. In a decrescendo, conversely, the brass and percussion should precede the strings and woodwind in cutting down the dynamic.

The physical technique of a crescendo in the winds, brasses, and percussion is generally understood and successfully executed, but there are many possibilities in string technique which are seldom fully exploited. The amount of bow-hair in contact with the string, the pressure of the bow on the string, and the speed with which the bow is drawn may all be increased as the crescendo progresses. The position of the bow may be changed from close to the finger board to a point as near the bridge as possible without producing a *sul ponticello* effect. This converts the string tone from soft diffusion to sharp intensity. Also, the width and rapidity of the vibrato may gradually be increased to advantage. This entire procedure works in reverse for a decrescendo.

Finally, care must be taken to see that the non-climactic crescendo-decrescendo within a phrase returns to the dynamic level at which it began. The problem with amateur players is to obtain a decrescendo to match the crescendo, for they will seldom return voluntarily to the point of dynamic departure. Failure to obtain this will result in a step-wise increase in sound with each successive execution of this effect.

Emotion

The techniques just outlined are but the incidental concomitants of interpretation, the trimming on the tree. If the conductor has done his work efficiently in the detailed rehearsals, the orchestra will have acquired technical confidence as its knowledge of the printed page has grown. But again technique is not enough. The conductor must now inspire in his players the same feeling for beauty, line, mood, and rhythm that characterizes his own conception of the music. As stated before, this cannot successfully be taught by rote. The players must know what they are doing and, more important still, why they are doing it. An artificial sort of beauty may occasionally be obtained from a group of amateur executants solely by the imposition of the conductor's emotional conceptions upon them, but this deprives the players of one of the finest musical experiences they could possibly have: active participation in the re-creative process. Only through the contribution of the players' own intelligence and emotion transmitted to the listener, may the performance achieve a sincerity and an integrity which will be persuasive.

This active participation may be obtained in a variety of ways, the most important of which are these: a careful explanation by the conductor of his mood objectives in each given passage and of the technical means by which the players can obtain those objectives; and the experiment of allowing the players to express a passage as they feel it, thus encouraging them to think about the emotional content of the music. A constructive critique of the results should foster a logical and satisfactory development of emotional sensitivity within the orchestra and do away with surface emotion as the dominant characteristic of the interpretive results. These techniques must be used over and over in the final rehearsals if they are to be effective. At first the results will be discouraging and far from the ideals of interpretation the conductor has in mind. With patience, persistence, imagination, and the expenditure of considerable ingenuity, the players *can* be stimulated to participate actively in the recreative process. I am fully aware that many will feel that this participation is impossible to attain with amateurs. All I can say is that I have seen it happen not once, but many times. A concert with this sort of training as a background can easily rise above mere adequacy and become an inspiration to the audience, the players, and the conductor alike. In making this possible, the conductor contributes greatly toward the development of his players, both as musicians and as persons.

VII

THE CONCERT

ONE of the principal objects of the meticulously planned rehearsal schedule previously outlined is to avoid the necessity of extra last-minute rehearsals, particularly on the day of the concert. Conductors will find that the stimulus of playing before an audience will postpone the approach of physical fatigue—but not if the players have been rehearsed right up until the eleventh hour. Nor is it good psychology to keep the audience waiting outside the doors of the concert hall while the proverbial nine stitches are being taken within. Now and then, circumstances may force the conductor to rehearse on the day of the concert: for example, a trip to an outside college or community for a joint concert with another orchestra or chorus, the late arrival of a guest conductor, or the inability of an out-of-town soloist to arrive before the day of the concert. In all of these cases, it is important that all concerned know their parts thoroughly in order that there may be a minimum of stopping for detailed drill. This is particularly true in the case of the guest conductor, for courtesy requires that the resident conductor shall prepare minutely the mechanical details, especially the notes, in such a way that the guest can, in his limited rehearsal time, concentrate on interpretation. In such extraordinary circumstances as these, the conductor should see to it that the rehearsal is as short and as free from tension as possible. In the case of the joint concert, it is a sound policy to rehearse only the beginnings and endings of the various numbers on the program, plus any difficult passages that may suggest themselves. In any event, it is essential that there be ample time for the players to rest between the rehearsal and the concert.

At least fifteen minutes in advance of the time set for the concert to begin, all members of the orchestra should be required to report to the tuning room for the purpose of warming up. If a keyboard instrument is to be used in the first part of the program, the concertmaster and the first oboe should adjust their pitch to it before tuning the orchestra. About ten minutes before the concert, all practicing should be stopped while the instruments are tuned. With orchestras in the older and more-experienced age groups, the preliminary tuning may well be left in the hands of the concertmaster and the leaders of the various sections, subject to a final check by the conductor. With younger and less-experienced players, the conductor should assume the tuning responsibility himself. No pains must be spared to see that each instrument is thoroughly and accurately tuned before the players go on the stage. Absolute silence on the part of all players not immediately concerned should be required during tuning by individuals or sections.

I have found it a good practice to speak briefly to the players before they leave the tuning room for the stage. The objectives are usually these: to remind them to watch the conductor closely at every possible moment and strive to obtain the utmost contrast in dynamics and mood; to check their collective memory for any repeat signs that are to be observed or omitted; to make certain that any required mutes are not being left behind and that there is a complete set of strings at the first stand of each string section. (This last precaution is very necessary when the weather is unseasonable, to avoid the distraction resulting from players dashing into the wings for emergency repairs.)

Naturally, the players should not be burdened with too many detailed instructions at this juncture. If the conductor confines himself to the essentials and delivers what he has to say with a discreet touch of humor here and there, he will not only accomplish his immediate purposes but will dissipate much of the pre-concert tension. This is an important factor in getting the concert off to a good start.

The players are sent on-stage five minutes or so before the scheduled time for the concert, and the concert should be begun on time. If the conductor acquires a reputation for starting promptly, his audiences will coöperate, particularly if they see the latecomers kept outside until the end of the first piece or movement. During the final rehearsals, the players are coached in stage deportment, especially on how to make a disciplined entrance without straggling and incidental byplay. Upon the arrival of the concertmaster, the pitch is given a short final check and the players then sit quietly awaiting the entrance of the conductor.

At the final rehearsal, the conductor has seen to it that the concert numbers are arranged in the correct order in each folder by the players themselves, and the librarian has since checked to see that no parts are missing. (It is suggested that no parts be allowed to be taken out between the final rehearsal and the concert. The danger is obvious.) The librarian has also placed a copy of the program on each stand, and the players now give this a final check against their own folders. If this is not done, the audience may be treated to simultaneous performances of two different works—as happened on one famous occasion in London when the strains of the Handel D-minor organ concerto mingled with the opening chords of the orchestral version of the "Hallelujah" chorus. This has to happen but once in a conductor's career to make him supersensitive on the subject of the correct order of music in the folders.

The players are also coached in advance regarding the importance of good posture, and must be given to understand that failure to observe it not only spoils the stage picture but also causes a loss in physical efficiency. They also know in advance whether or not they may leave the stage during the playing of any score not requiring their services. Any reseating of the orchestra for a number involving a soloist is explained in detail at the dress rehearsal. In short, every effort must be made to ensure the smooth and efficient running of the concert once it is under way. Nothing will cause the audience to become restless more quickly than confusion or indecision on the stage or long waits between numbers.

Before the conductor enters from the wings, it is wise for him to take a quick glance over his forces and see that no essential performer is absent. This happens now and then, even with professionals. At a certain performance of the Brahms "Requiem," the conductor had entered and even raised his arms for the opening chord before he discovered that the baritone soloist was not in his place. There ensued an embarrassing interim of some ten minutes until the lost sheep was found and returned to the fold. It developed that he had forgotten to set his watch to conform to daylight saving time. The applause at his belated entrance was tumultuous, but did not exactly help to set the serious mood needed for a performance of the "Requiem."

Once the conductor has stepped out on the stage, he must subject himself to the same sort of discipline he requires of his players. He should make his entrance in a dignified but businesslike manner and take his place on the podium with as little delay and as few caracoles as possible. As soon as he has the attention of the orchestra and the audience, he should raise the baton—but not before. A lengthy pose with upraised arms, however effective from the audience viewpoint, will only serve to create tension and uncertainty among the players. It also allows them to see how shaky the conductor's hands are, and nervousness is the most communicable of all concert ailments!

Sir Adrian Boult has aptly said that the work of the conductor should be directed toward the eyes of the orchestra and only toward the ears of the audience. This modest concept is decidedly not in vogue in present day professional circles, but anything less than a careful adherence to it will turn an amateur concert into a ludicrous spectacle. Violent gymnastics and facial grimaces suggestive of a soul in torment must be avoided at all costs. The air surrounding the podium should not be flagellated, even in the most stirring climaxes; nor should the podium be used as an area for constant, albeit restricted, strolling from one section of the orchestra to another. Rhythmic effects should be handled by the percussion section alone, and the conductor should not supplement their efforts by beating audible time with one or both feet. The conducting stand, moreover, should not be used as a large-scale metronome. And last, but far from least, the conductor must not sing. This form of self-expression should be limited to the privacy of the rehearsal and the shower.

On the positive side, the gestures of the conductor should always be in keeping with the mood and dynamics of the moment; their scope and character must bear a direct relation to the sound being produced by the orchestra. I am not suggesting that the conductor obliterate himself from the stage picture, but merely that he should so discipline himself in the quieter passages that it will not be necessary for him to call into play his hair, cuffs, and coat-tails to make an impression in the climaxes. In short, he ought not to obtrude himself between the audience and the music but should try, with every legitimate visual means at his command, to deepen the listeners' insight into the inner meaning of the music. The conductor's bodily motion on the podium should be strictly limited, and there should be a definite pivoting point which he seldom, if ever, leaves. It is an effective technique to turn slightly toward a section of the orchestra which is about to have something musically important to say, but even this should not be overdone.

The possession of an expressive and efficient left (or nonbaton) hand is a prime necessity for any conductor. Too often the left hand is used merely as a mirror of the right, exercising no independent function of its own. It should be free to control the various dynamic changes in the score, to give cues, and to indicate the conductor's desires with regard to balance between the various sections of the orchestra. The matter of giving cues needs to be enlarged upon, for it is a subject of the greatest importance to the conductor of the amateur orchestra. If the players are trained to expect and to respond to numerous cues, the conductor's control over his forces will be increased and the players will derive added confidence from the knowledge that they may depend on him in case of any lapses due to faulty counting or loss of place. Only by constant control of this sort can a player making a false entry be waved out or a player missing an entry be brought in. The two hands are used as one unit, in general, only in reinforcing climaxes and in securing unanimous attacks and releases. There are two additional observations to be made before leaving this subject: (1) There are moments when the left hand may well be in repose. (2) A conductor is no more effective than his left hand.

Good posture on the podium is as important as it is in the orchestra. The conductor should stand erect, with head held high and shoulders back. The relation of the music stand to good posture has already been mentioned and need not be repeated here. The planes in which the baton moves must be visible to the players at all times. Particular care must be taken to see that the down-beat does not go below the level of the score, nor the up-beat above the conductor's head. It must always be borne in mind that the players need to be able to locate and identify the beat at a glance, for they cannot afford to lose more than momentary contact with the printed page. The beat, therefore, must be governed by the prevailing sight lines from the players to the podium.

The conductor should employ the motions of his right hand in direct proportion to the indicated dynamic, progressing from the small patterns of the fingers and wrist alone to the forearm and finally to the upper arm. Under no circumstances should the shoulders be raised. This gesture is ineffective, awkward, and causes the tails of a dress coat to open and shut like a pair of scissors. Two final don'ts on the subject of posture: don't ever bend the knees; and don't give the appearance of brooding over the score by falling victim to "conductor's stoop."

The conducting needs to be so clear and unequivocal that there is no possibility that the audience will break into thunderous applause when the orchestra merely pauses for a G.P. or a hold. A number of symphonic works contain audience-traps of this sort which the conductor must help his listeners to avoid. Similarly, the cut-off at the end of a movement or of a work must be clear and distinct, especially if the work is unfamiliar to the audience. Indecision in these cases usually arises when the ending is quiet and the last chord involves a decrescendo hold. I suggest that the cut-off be made with both hands slightly higher than customary and in full view of the audience. If need be, the conductor can reinforce this by stepping down from the podium. I realize that the prevailing conducting technique is to hide such a cut-off with all the care of a conjurer palming an egg, and this does, I admit, produce a tense, theatrical silence that impresses the musically naïve among the listeners. It also has its dangers when attempted with amateurs. I once played in a concert where the ensuing silence went on and on until it was broken by some good Samaritan saying, in clear, ringing tones: "Oh come on, let's give them a hand!" And so the day was saved.

It is a gracious gesture to have the players stand to share the applause with the conductor at least twice during the concert program: just before the intermission and at the end of the concert. If this is done after every number, it tends to become a meaningless formality. In any event, the players must be coached in advance to rise together, and without straggling, on the conductor's signal. They should also be trained to stand without fidget-

ing once they are on their feet. A final item of pre-
concert coaching on stage discipline is that the orchestra
will not leave until it is given a prearranged signal by the
concertmaster. It is not good manners to walk out while
the audience is still applauding.

Before leaving the subject of the concert, I would like
to consolidate the salient points about the program itself:
(1) The program of a concert by an amateur orchestra
should not be too long, for it is far better to send the audience away wanting to hear more than it is to test its
powers of endurance to the breaking point. (2) The program should be planned in such a way that the works
demanding the most concentrated listening come while
the audience (and the orchestra) are freshest. (3) Concerts should be begun promptly and run off expeditiously.
(4) Long waits between numbers should be avoided, and
the conductor should not parade on and off the stage
after each one except for the purpose of escorting a soloist to his place before the orchestra. (5) Under certain
circumstances, an intermission may be dispensed with to
advantage. Examples of the latter might be a late afternoon concert or a program involving some resetting of
the stage for a soloist. Often at a late afternoon concert,
expediency may suggest the omission of an intermission.
Again, when a stage must be reset for a soloist, this
interval gives the audience ample opportunity to relax
and so makes an additional respite superfluous.

The interest and enjoyment of the audience are stimulated and increased through the use of program notes.
These may be either printed notes in the program or oral
notes given by the conductor. In certain respects the
latter are to be preferred at an amateur concert, for
the spoken word, if well chosen, helps to break down the

formal atmosphere and puts both the audience and the orchestra at ease. Written program notes may well be prepared by some qualified member (or members) of the orchestra. One college orchestra in New England enlists the aid of the music history class, to their mutual profit. If the notes are spoken, they should be informative, witty without being flippant, and brief.

VIII

ORCHESTRAL BASIC TRAINING

DISCIPLINE, in the restrictive and punitive sense of the word, should have to play a very small part in the training of an amateur orchestra. The conductor can cut his disciplinary problems to a minimum in two ways: (1) by developing his rehearsal technique to the point where the players are kept too interested and too busy to find time for extracurricular byplay; (2) by seeing to it that no breach of the orchestral peace passes unnoticed. By working persistently along these parallel lines, the conductor can eventually achieve complete control of the rehearsals. It is obvious what this control means to the development of the orchestra as a whole and to its preparation of the individual concert.

Orchestras of young players invariably contain certain overexuberant spirits whose excess energy needs constantly to be guided into constructive channels. In dealing with such early disciplinary problems as these people pose, the conductor must be firm, just, and tactful. He must *never* lose his temper. Self-control comes first; then control over others will follow.

Discipline in the broadest sense of the word is the foundation of any successful group enterprise. In the orchestral field, one of the earliest concerns of the conductor must be to train the players to arrive promptly at rehearsals, for much irreplaceable practice time can be lost through tardiness. The conductor should make clear his desire for punctuality at the first rehearsal. Having stated a policy of starting promptly at the announced rehearsal time, he must maintain it. Actions here speak much louder than words, and a rigid adherence to this policy (no matter how many players are on stage ready to begin) will bear fruit in time. Those who continue to be noncoöperative should be seen individually by the conductor. One astute person of my acquaintance converts the tardy with the public greeting: "Ah! the late Mr. ————!" Some organizations close the doors of the rehearsal hall promptly at the appointed hour, and the latecomers are not admitted until the first pause in the rehearsal schedule. The publicity attendant upon the late entrance in this case is considerable, and is often accentuated by spontaneous hissing from the other members of the group. A system of fines for tardiness or absence is hardly compatible with the amateur ideal; in addition, it is a tacit admission of the inability of the conductor and the officers to cope with the situation in any other way. It is far better to obtain the support of the membership through interest and natural enthusiasm than through any form of compulsion or penalty. In cases where academic credit is given for instrumental ensemble participation, the conductor has an artificial control over the players, but this substitutes self-interest for the healthier motivation of natural loyalty.

There must be an understanding at the outset of the season regarding the importance of regular attendance at rehearsals. It must be stressed that nothing will retard the development of the orchestra more than poor attendance. The handicap imposed by missing players in the wind, brass, and percussion sections will be obvious to all concerned, but a special point will need to be made for the string players. One player out of ten or twelve violins, for example, will reason that his presence or absence makes little or no difference. It is not difficult to show that the lack of knowledge of what takes place during his absence may easily mean that the instruction will have to be repeated for his special benefit at the next rehearsal. The development of the section as a unit can be seriously impeded by absences within the membership.

It should be explained that only the most valid reasons for absence will be accepted by the conductor and the officers, and that excessive absence will mean dismissal from the orchestra. The Harvard University Orchestra requires that written excuses be submitted to the secretary in advance of the absence, countersigned by the conductor. Absences for unforeseen reasons are similarly treated, post facto. There is also an announced policy regarding the exact number of absences a player may have each semester during the school year and still remain a member of the orchestra. A certain number of latenesses is considered equal to one absence. Apart from the value of such a policy in developing a sense of responsibility in the individual toward the group as a whole, it enables the conductor to plan his rehearsals more efficiently through his advance knowledge of what players and instruments will not be available at a given rehearsal.

Good posture at rehearsals is as important as it is at concerts, and for the same reasons. The players must be trained to sit up straight in their chairs and to hold their instruments in the approved manner. They must not be allowed to slump down, cross their knees, or perch their feet on the chair in front of them.

Keeping time by beating the foot on the floor must not be permitted. If the individual player feels that he needs the moral support of this artificial aid, he must be taught to move the foot *inside* the shoe.

The conductor should train himself never to raise the baton in rehearsal until he is ready to have the orchestra play. To save time, he must have an instantaneous response to this gesture from his players. Nothing will impair the rapidity of this response more than to have the baton go up and then come right down again because the conductor has thought of some additional pearl of wisdom he wishes to cast. As a corollary to this, the orchestra should be trained to obey instantly the signal to stop playing, for the universal tendency of the amateur is to continue playing for five or six bars after the signal. Countless valuable minutes of rehearsal time can be lost in this way. During the early rehearsals, when the orchestra is concentrating on unfamiliar music, this signal can be an aural one: a repeated tapping on the conductor's stand, or a clapping of the hands. Later on, the orchestra should be expected to respond to a visual cut-off as part of their training in watching the conductor. A cut-off must not be allowed to be construed as a signal for extemporaneous playing, nor an invitation to commence social conversation. Careful training in these seemingly minor matters will save literally hours of rehearsal time over the course of a season.

If the instructions the conductor wishes to give are for a specific section or an individual player, he should insist that those not specifically concerned maintain complete silence. At times, the other players may well be asked to follow along on their own parts and pay careful attention to the points being made.

The players should be encouraged to ask questions of the conductor, especially when they are not quite clear on a point he is trying to impress upon them. Again, this is a device aimed at saving time. The conductor who does not encourage questions from his players will find himself forced to repeat and repeat his instructions before the desired result is obtained. No matter how hectic the rehearsal may be at a given moment, the conductor should do his best to answer a question as fully and as clearly as possible. In time, the number of questions he is asked will be a barometer of the players' interest and enthusiasm.

Nothing so disrupts the concentration required at rehearsals as players wandering on and off the stage at odd intervals. The players should be required to obtain the conductor's permission in advance of any change of base while the rehearsal is in progress. A constant sense of responsibility to a central authority is of vital importance in the establishment and maintenance of good discipline.

Players should be encouraged to take music out for private practice, but this immediately poses certain problems of organization. How is this music to be signed out and checked in? The Harvard University Orchestra requires that the music be taken to the librarian and that a charge slip, made out and signed, be left with him; the music is returned in the same way, before the starting time of the next rehearsal. The New England Conservatory Orchestra has a number of library slips in a special pocket in every folder. The player signs the music out himself, but signs it in through the librarian. It must be understood that music taken out *must* be back for the next rehearsal. Work on a specific piece may be badly hampered by the absence of one part, particularly if a duplicate is not available. If the player finds that he cannot, for some unforeseen reason, attend the next rehearsal, he is still responsible for finding some means of getting the music.

back. The conductor must, out of fairness to the whole orchestra, be severe with infractions of this rule.

The value of humor in lightening the necessarily businesslike and concentrated atmosphere of the rehearsal cannot be underestimated. Humor, if well-timed, brief, and apt, can drive home a point in more lasting fashion than almost any other teaching device. It also affords the relaxing experience of a hearty laugh. The orchestra needs these moments, together with a mid-rehearsal rest period, if it is to stand up under the intense physical and mental effort required of it. The conductor may often receive assistance along these lines, unconsciously or otherwise, from the players themselves. This should be encouraged, but only up to a point. Humor at the wrong place or at the wrong time can be subversive of good discipline. Close watch needs to be kept over the inevitable player-comedian whose sense of humor is better than his timing.

All criticism of the work of individual players must be constructive, for it is very bad psychology to humiliate an amateur player before his colleagues by destructive criticism or, worst of all, by sarcasm. The only time the conductor has any justification for being severe in his approach to a player is when the playing is unintelligent, non-coöperative, or shows inattention to instructions. An alert group of players should not make the same mistake twice, once they have been taught how to avoid making it. A recurrence is then indicative of a lack of concentration. The players should be urged to make a new mistake, if they must, but not repeat the old.

Every amateur orchestra contains a number of overcautious members whose main ambition in life seems to be to conceal their errors not only from the conductor but even from their immediate neighbors. The mental approach of these players is completely false. They believe that by blowing gently into their instruments, or by utilizing an absolute minimum of bow, their sins of omission and commission will pass unnoticed. In the first place, this is usually an erroneous assumption; in the second, such players might just as well be out in the audience for all they are contributing to the general orchestral effect. Their very air of unobtrusiveness marks them from the podium, and eventually from the audience. The conductor has to keep after these people to redouble their efforts on behalf of the orchestra, and must impress upon them that if there is to be a mistake, he wants a good one. Let there be no doubt anywhere in the hall that a "clinker" has occurred. Unless every single player can be taught to play with enthusiasm and a certain amount of what may be termed controlled abandon, the orchestral tone will never have vitality, breadth, or depth.

These various disciplines will have to be restated and enforced many times before they become thoroughly ingrained in the players, but the effort required will soon bear fruit in abundance. Better results will be obtained from each successive rehearsal, group spirit and morale will increase, and greater success will be attained in concert. The patience of the conductor will inevitably be taxed to the utmost, but the results will more than justify the means.

IX

ORGANIZATION

THE support of an enthusiastic and efficient group of officers can be of the greatest assistance to the conductor of
an amateur orchestra. His ability to secure the coöperation of these leaders and his willingness to delegate authority and responsibility to them may well determine the
degree of success he may expect with the orchestra as an
organization. Naturally, the scope of the work of the officers will vary greatly with the age-group involved. But
the conductor owes it to his players to allow those qualified to assume some degree of responsibility and learn
how to discharge it to the best of their ability. This is
probably the most important contribution he can make
to their development as responsible persons.

An orchestra is too complex an organism to be run
successfully as a one-man show. The conductor should
try to free himself of all responsibility, save that of advisor, in areas not directly concerned with the development and training of the orchestra as a musical unit. This
will create a strong central nucleus of leadership, and
since the officers in turn will be elected by the membership of the orchestra, all will feel that they have a voice
and an interest in its affairs above and beyond their status
as players.

One of the main functions of the officers as a group

will be to act as a liaison between the conductor and the personnel of the orchestra. By this means the conductor is able to keep his finger on the pulse of the orchestra to learn its state of mind and the condition of its morale. He can also obtain valuable information regarding the efficiency of his training methods and the degree of interest aroused by his choice of repertory. If the conductor is willing to listen to constructive criticism, he can learn almost as much from his players as they do from him. In any event, the free flow of ideas from the players to the conductor through this channel creates a healthy atmosphere within the orchestra.

Another important function of the officers can be to take charge of the social activities of the orchestra. Naturally, the main purpose of the players is to make music together, but nothing will further the development of the necessary group solidarity more than an occasional social affair completely apart from the concentrated and purposeful atmosphere of the rehearsals. Mentioned previously as devices for launching the orchestral season have been the sight-reading evening, with refreshments and a social hour at the end, the tea, and the luncheon. The officers of the various orchestras which have initiated these events have also held dances after formal concerts, Christmas parties, picnics, and annual banquets with prominent guest speakers from the musical world. These are but some of the possibilities for getting the players better acquainted and for developing the orchestra as a corporate entity.

The officers can also be a great help to the conductor in discovering and ferreting out instrumental talent in the school or the community. There will always be a certain number of qualified players who, for one reason or another, do not present themselves when the tryouts and auditions are held. They may be overmodest about their own capabilities, or may have missed the orchestra's public announcements of the opening of the season. Among school and college students, there may be some who are doubtful of their ability to carry a full academic schedule and still participate in an extracurricular activity. The officers are in a better position to seek these people out and interest them in the orchestra than is the conductor.

In a community orchestra, it is a good policy to have an advisory committee chosen from among interested townspeople to work with the conductor and the officers. A broader base of active interest and support is required here than in the school and college orchestra.

The following description of the possible duties of the various officers combines the best features of the two systems with which I have had experience. A great deal, needless to say, depends on the caliber of the officeholders themselves and on the absence of politics in their choice. The conductor must do everything he possibly can to discourage electioneering, the intrusion of fraternity or sorority politics, or the development of well-organized minority cliques.

President (elected): to work closely with the conductor in every phase of the orchestra's activities save in the choice of program material and the conduct of rehearsals; to preside over all meetings of the orchestra and of the officers, both of which should be held at regularly stated intervals; to relieve the conductor of as many cares connected with the management of the orchestra as possible; to choose assisting committees, as needed, from the membership at large.

Vice-President (elected): to assist the president in the above duties; to carry out his functions in the former's absence; to have charge of all publicity connected with the activities of the orchestra, both musical and social; to keep a permanent record of programs, reviews, and published material of all sorts.

Treasurer (elected): to take charge of the financial affairs of the orchestra; to keep accounts; to render periodic reports; to receive and send out bills; and to try to balance the budget.

Secretary (elected): to take attendance at rehearsals; to keep minutes of the business meetings of the orchestra and of the officers; to take charge of all correspondence not in the province of the other officers.

Manager (appointed): to schedule concerts and to make all the necessary arrangements for them; to secure transportation for trips; to post all details regarding rehearsal and concert dates; to set up the stage; to supervise all the physical assets of the orchestra except the library. The manager, and his assistants, are appointed by the conductor and the other officers after a competition lasting over a certain stated number of months. This procedure is more likely to insure the choice of an efficient and capable person for this key position than the elective process.

Librarian (appointed). Good librarians are born, not made. An efficient person in this key position can make a great deal of difference to the smooth functioning of rehearsals and concerts. The person chosen must have a natural flair for library work, and must be willing to take the meticulous care needed to keep his department in complete order. He is responsible for making up the folders at the beginning of the season, for putting them out at each rehearsal, and for keeping them in order at all times; he checks the music out for practice and checks it in at the next rehearsal; he must constantly be alert to

prevent the loss of parts, to track them down when they
go astray, and to replace them when they are irretrievably
lost; he keeps the music in good condition by mending it
when it starts to become worn; he keeps the card catalogue
up to date and returns scores and parts to the library
when the orchestra is through with them; he is also
responsible for putting bowings, fingerings, and phrase
markings in the parts as required by the conductor. This
is a taxing position and one of cardinal importance in the
orchestral chain of command. A good librarian can do
much to help the conductor preserve his sanity!

With the advice and help of the conductor, the officers
can be trained to handle most of the details connected
with the giving of a public concert. This includes publicity, planning the ticket selling campaign (with the active help of *all* the members of the orchestra), organiz-
ing the word-of-mouth advertising so helpful to an amateur orchestra, and having the posters, programs, and
tickets printed and distributed. All of the work connected
with the concert should be planned in such a way as to
enlist the active support of as many members of the
orchestra as possible. This is partly for the purpose of
dividing the burden equally, partly for the purpose of
solidifying group spirit, but mainly in order to avoid any
feeling among the general membership that the officers
are constituting themselves a small but powerful ruling
clique.

At the end of each season, the conductor will do well
to sit down with his officers in an informal atmosphere
for a frank discussion both pro and con of every phase of
the season. If the conductor encourages the utmost frank-
ness in the expression of individual opinion, he will have
a chance to see himself as a musician and teacher through

the eyes of his players. In addition, he will quickly discover what aspects of his training methods are most successful, and what aspects will bear improving. He will find out what sort of music his players enjoy most and what they like least. In this regard, he need not fear the musical tastes of his officers; not if his own are sound. They may express a desire to play the Franck symphony or the Tschaikovsky Fifth, for the amateur's ambitions almost always exceed his technical ability; but I doubt that they will clamor for the "Poet and Peasant" overture or "In a Monastery Garden."

No conductor will ever find himself in a rut if he takes advantage of these periodic opportunities to see himself as his players see him, and if he is responsive to the impact of constructive new ideas on the organization and running of the orchestra.

SIGHT READING

In considering the subject of orchestral sight reading, we come face to face with a strange paradox: the most important skill that an instrumentalist can possess, outside of the mastery of his instrument, receives the least emphasis in his early training. No matter what phase of amateur or professional music the player may elect to pursue in later life, the ability to read creditably at sight is a vital necessity. It is one of the first prerequisites for success in any form of professional ensemble work, it contributes materially to the development of the amateur orchestra, and it is the keystone of amateur chamber music making. Yet the opportunities for practice in sight reading are at present so limited that scarcely one player in five is able to pass a college or conservatory test in it. Most of those who do pass such tests have acquired their skill through home-sponsored chamber music and not through what should be the normal channel, the student orchestra. The question reduces itself to this: Should not amateur orchestras, particularly those composed of elementary school and high-school age students, provide more opportunities for experience in sight reading? To my mind, there can be but one answer.

The reason why conductors do not feel that they can afford to devote valuable rehearsal time to this work is understandable, but not entirely justifiable. Briefly, it is the pressure of having to produce periodic concerts after only a limited number of rehearsals. A more pernicious pressure is exerted by the glorified musical track meet known as the state or regional contest. With his job often at stake, the conductor naturally feels he must concentrate on the contest music to the exclusion of sight reading. Experience has shown many times, however, that systematic training in sight reading, in brief but regular periods, yields dividends to the orchestra and to the individual player out of all proportion to the actual amount of time invested. In a very short while the conductor will find that his players are acquiring a facility in reading that enables them to progress faster and further in rehearsals available. Less time has to be spent in learning the notes; the reading rehearsals previously discussed are more satisfactory; the detailed rehearsals are more efficient, and may even be reduced in number; and the final results cannot help but be a distinct advance over anything the orchestra has previously achieved.

There are several ways in which practice in sight reading may be incorporated into the regular rehearsal schedule. Most teachers of orchestral conducting recommend that each rehearsal begin with a warm-up piece. This worth-while device can be combined with sight reading by the use of an unfamiliar march, overture, movement of a symphony, or a short piece. Five or six minutes of playing time is usually sufficient to get the players in fine fettle for the main work of the rehearsal. In addition to limbering up the orchestra, this device accomplishes two other important ends: (1) It stimulates the players' interest in the work of the orchestra by affording them an opportunity to combine sight-reading practice with increasing their knowledge of the orchestral literature outside of the repertory of their particular group. (2) It is a deterrent of tardiness, for once the idea takes shape, the players will not want to miss the fun and experience afforded by this new phase of their training.

The Harvard University Orchestra developed its sight-reading program to the point where the first fifteen minutes of each rehearsal, except just before a concert, were devoted exclusively to it. In one semester, the orchestra read four symphonies, the Beethoven 1st and 7th, and the Mozart G minor and E flat, as well as a number of overtures and ballet suites. The symphonies were read at the rate of one movement per rehearsal.

The works chosen must be carefully related to the collective ability and experience of the group in question. This is most important in the beginning, as poor results at this juncture will destroy the idea before it has time to take root. The grade of difficulty may be increased as the players acquire greater fluency in reading. The conductor can stimulate the active interest of the orchestra by accepting requests for a sight reading of certain works during the course of the year. These will need to be carefully watched, for the players will invariably want to attempt Brahms before they have mastered Haydn!

Sight reading may also be introduced into the orchestral season by devoting an entire rehearsal to it immediately after a public concert. This procedure is psychologically sound as it helps to counteract the inevitable letdown after a concert for which the players have worked hard over a considerable period of time. It turns the orchestra out to pasture, so to speak, before beginning work on a new program. The schedule of concerts for the New England Conservatory Orchestra is so planned that at least two weeks are available for nothing but sight reading between the December concert and the Christmas

vacation. This is in addition to a regular orchestra reading class which meets two hours a week for the school
year. I cite this to emphasize the importance a professional school places on this phase of orchestral training.
The added efficiency of this orchestra in its second-semes-
ter concerts is marked, and much of it can be attributed
directly to the experience it gains during this period.

About ten years ago, the Harvard Orchestra inaugu-
rated the custom of beginning and ending its concert season with an open sight-reading evening. At these affairs,
the orchestra plays host to all interested amateur players
in the area of metropolitan Boston. Invitations are ex-
tended by means of announcements in the public press,
by posters in the various schools and colleges, and by
postcards to the large mailing list which has been built
up over the years. The general rule is that no one will be
admitted unless accompanied by an instrument, but an
audience usually gathers just the same.

The size of the orchestra at these sight readings has
grown from an initial 55 to a record 157 in 1947 that
taxed the facilities of the Sanders Theatre stage to the
utmost. The players are allowed to seat themselves wherever they feel they can be the most efficient and have the
most fun. Only a few key players are assigned seats by
the conductor. The instrumentation has shown a gradual
evolution, and from limited and oddly-balanced beginnings, has now reached a point where it lacks only two
instruments (contra-bassoon and bass clarinet) of the
modern symphony orchestra. Of course, there are always
more flutes, clarinets, trumpets, and horns than one can
shake a baton at, but given sufficient strings to balance
them, this only adds to the fun. A purist would undoubtedly shudder at the thought of the Scherzo from Mendelssohn's "Midsummer Night's Dream" with 14 flutes,

or the slow movement from Tschaikovsky's 5th symphony with 15 horns. But purists are barred from the sessions, which are by, for, and of amateurs.

The nucleus of the orchestra is drawn from Harvard, Radcliffe, Wellesley, and the New England Conservatory. The other players are bona fide amateurs of all hues and degrees of ability from the preparatory schools, high schools, and the general highways and byways of musical Boston. They range all the way from teen-agers to a staid member of the Massachusetts Supreme Court.

Rudolph Elie Jr., music critic of the *Boston Herald,* attended one of these sight-reading sessions in 1942 and wrote an unusually discerning review of it. He so completely caught the spirit and purpose of the idea that I would like to quote excerpts from his article as a summing up of one aspect of the case for more sight reading among amateurs.

"There was a meeting last week—the final one of the year—of the 'Harvard Society for Sight Reading Symphonic Stuff' and, after a long season of concert-going in which precision of performance was the advertised if not always forthcoming feature, we ventured out to Sanders Theatre for the sheer novelty of expecting to hear music sound a great deal better than its performers said it would, and not, as is more often the case, vice versa.

"Although these wonderful sight readings have been going on at Harvard for some time now and do not then constitute spectacular musical news, we enjoyed ourselves so much that we can't resist reporting the event and pointing a slight moral. The plan, actually, is very simple. It seems that anybody who has achieved a moderate technique on an orchestral instrument is invited to bring himself, his music stand, and his instrument to Sanders Theatre at the appointed hour. He is given a seat and the music of an orchestral piece the name of which is not revealed to him until he takes his place, so he can't of course cheat by practicing the part beforehand.

"Mr. Holmes conducts the sight reading. His only rules are that everybody must play in the same key and that everybody must begin at the same time; even these rules may be—and often are—suspended.

"The other night the program turned out to consist of the Mozart 'Haffner' and the Brahms 1st symphonies, neither of which by any means allows the instrumentalist to doze in his rests.

"We need not linger over the musical products of the ensemble by remarking on its sonorities or the hues of its tonal palette, or discuss the various styles of foot-tapping in evidence. The fact of the matter is, it was astonishingly good sight reading and—what is more important and more to the point—it was good fun for the player and the auditor alike. It must not be assumed, however, that because it was fun, it was frivolous.

"On the contrary, the potential musicianship of the ensemble was everywhere apparent. The conductor, on his side, shouted advice and encouragement with good-humored insight into the problems and states-of-mind of his musicians, while they, in turn, responded to his suggestions without a trace of self-consciousness. In short, the music they made represented musical self-expression in one of its purest aspects.

"Frankly, we had much rather listen to ten of these sight-reading sessions than to hear one concert by ultra-skilled musicians who are bored beyond endurance. Deliver us from musicians whose aversion to music is painfully apparent and from musical audiences who believe that all music is a sort of rite to be approached with set and slightly paled faces.

"Obviously, we are not pleading any relaxation in musical standards; on the contrary. Any musician knows that sight-reading is one thing, audience performance another. But is it too much to ask them to capture some of the joy and exaltation of performance of music that this sight-reading session so exuberantly demonstrated the other night?"

The overtures for these evenings have ranged from "Prometheus" to "Die Meistersinger"; the symphonies, from the "London" of Haydn to the Brahms 4th; and the third work, from ballet suites by Gretry and Rameau, to Handel *concerti grossi* and the Bach 3rd Brandenburg concerto. As the group has grown in size and developed in ability, the repertory has become broader in scope and more ambitious in character.

It is made clear to the players before the evening gets under way that, since the object is to sight read for the fun and experience of it, no stops will be made unless the situation becomes musically hopeless. If a player loses his place, he is expected to get back in again on his own, with only minor help from his nearest neighbor and from the conductor—who calls out the letters or numbers in the score as they fly by. The only coaching done by the conductor before the actual playing begins is to point out any major changes of key, tempo, or time signature that may occur during the course of the work or movement to be played. An agreement is also reached regarding the observance or nonobservance of repeat marks or first and second endings. A special point has to be made concerning the *da capo* of a minuet, lest the unwary go blithely on into the next movement.

During the actual playing, the conductor uses every means at his command to keep the players together and the tempo steady. He also does his best to obtain at least a superficial adherence to dynamic indications. As the players become experienced in sight reading, more can be expected of them. The conductor should never give the impression that he is satisfied merely to get through a number at an unwavering forte, and without a breakdown. This is the first objective, but not the final one.

As in the concert program, the hardest number should come early in the evening and should be followed by an intermission. The point has been made that these evenings are devoid of any semblance of rehearsing. However, as more ambitious works are attempted, this rule is occasionally waived for the purpose of going over a difficult passage once or twice at a slow tempo. Quite often an overture or movement of a symphony is repeated at the request of the players themselves or at the suggestion of the conductor.

There is no more effective nor pleasant way of launching a new orchestra in a school or a community than by means of one of these sight-reading evenings. With a thorough publicity campaign and a well-chosen program of music to read, the conductor can count on attracting the attendance of interested instrumentalists. During the course of the evening, he will have ample opportunity to demonstrate his musicianship, to communicate his enthusiasm for the new project, and to enlist the support of those who attend.

The Harvard Musical Association in Boston formed an orchestra in 1947 by means of a series of four sight-reading evenings held at biweekly intervals. This is perhaps the purest expression of the amateur ideal in orchestral playing: the making of music together for the sheer fun of becoming acquainted at first hand with the best in symphonic literature, and at the same time enjoying the freedom which comes from the realization that public performance is not anticipated. The response from adult players, most of them members of the Association who have not lost their undergraduate enthusiasm for instrumental music, was such that the orchestra is now on a permanent basis. It has a biweekly sight-reading evening on Friday nights from October to May, with a repertory that is constantly changing and expanding.

The New England Conservatory has recently sponsored an even more ambitious form of sight reading by inviting its student body and the general public to spend one noon hour a month singing (at sight) great choral masterpieces to the accompaniment (also at sight) of the Conservatory Orchestra. The first two meetings in this series were devoted to the Brahms "Requiem" with student soloists. Another series featured the choruses from the Bach B-minor Mass. These meetings are open to the entire student body, not just to voice majors or to the Conservatory Chorus. The response to this innovation was so gratifying that it is being continued with a repertory including the Handel Messiah, Brahms's "Nanie" and "Schicksalslied," Haydn's "The Seasons," and the Bach "St. Matthew Passion."

Before leaving this subject, it should be reiterated that the gains from this sort of training are cumulative. The regularity with which the players are exposed to sight reading is of the utmost importance. An occasional period devoted to it will provide a bit of relaxation, but not much else. The conductor of an amateur orchestra cannot afford to overlook the potential benefits latent in an organized program of sight reading—benefits both to the individual and to the orchestra as a whole. It would be difficult to think of any consideration or situation which would lead me to omit this most necessary phase of an amateur player's training.

XI

ADDITIONAL SOURCES OF ORCHESTRAL REPERTORY

GOETHE has said: "The greatest respect an artist can show his public consists in never offering what people expect, but rather what he considers proper and useful at the given stage of his own development and that of his public." This could become a fine credo for the conductor of an amateur orchestra by the simple addition of a clause referring to the stage of development of his players.

The amateur orchestra has failed to achieve what should be its unique place in the musical pattern of our time because conductors have too often contented themselves with aping the programs of professional orchestras. Box-office considerations exert a powerful influence on the latter to give the public what it expects from a well-worn standard repertory. In taking the professional program as a model, the conductor of the amateur orchestra succeeds in producing only an inadequate facsimile, devoid of an integrity and purpose of its own. This is all the more regrettable because it could so easily be avoided by the use of a little imagination and resourcefulness in choosing the amateur repertory.

Granted that the community orchestra has an obligation to its listeners to acquaint them with the masterworks of the standard orchestral literature, particularly where the community is distant from a metropolitan center and the services of a professional symphony orchestra; granted, too, that elementary school, high-school, and college orchestras have an obligation to familiarize their players with such of these masterworks as may lie within the scope of their technical ability; nevertheless, the increased amount of fine symphonic music available on the radio and the development of music appreciation courses in the schools are more than sufficient to release both groups from their present preoccupation with conventional orchestral fare. The community orchestra might well reduce the percentage of standard works while increasing the percentage of new and unfamiliar music; the school or college orchestra could achieve its objectives by the occasional presentation of standard works on its public programs and the frequent use of them in sight-reading practice.

This brings us face to face with the necessity of defining the field in which the amateur orchestra *can* achieve an individuality of its own and still make a contribution to the musical growth of its players and its audiences. What is there left for it to explore? First, there is a vast store of material by both reputable and little-known composers from every period of musical history which has not attracted the professional orchestras or, in many cases, the publishers, because much of it is in the smaller forms or calls for limited instrumentation. Also, much of this music features simplicity and directness to the exclusion of the emotional bathos and the stupendous physical climaxes which seem to be the necessary concomitants of commercial and artistic success in the twentieth century.

This unexploited orchestral material exists in several forms: a great deal of it is to be found only in published

editions of the complete works of the several composers
or in collections illustrating the development of instrumental music by periods; an even larger amount of it
exists only in manuscript form in libraries and private
collections both in America and in Europe.

As examples of the first of these categories, the complete works of Haydn and Mozart are often the sole
printed source of the lesser-known symphonies, concertos,
and instrumental works of these men; the complete operas
of Handel, Gretry, Rameau, and Purcell contain many
fine overtures and dance movements not available separately. Among the most important of the collections are
the German, Austrian, and Bavarian Denkmälers. These
invaluable volumes contain, for example, works from the
Mannheim School, which played such an important part
in the development of instrumental music. The tracking
down of manuscripts is a fascinating pursuit and one that
is most rewarding in every way.

There are several guides to individual research which
will prove most helpful. The first of these is a handbook
entitled *Catalogue of Music for Small Orchestra* by Sal-
tonstall and Smith, published by the Music Library Association, Music Division of the Library of Congress. Its
value to the conductor of an amateur orchestra is im-
measurable, for it lists hundreds of works, both published and unpublished, which are ideal for the group
limited in instrumentation or in technical ability. The
instrumentation is given in each instance, often the performing time, and always the publisher or the source
where the work may be found. The indices are note-
worthy as timesavers for the conductor, as each work
is listed by composer, by title, and by instrumentation
(two winds with strings, three winds with strings, and
so on).

For the conductor who can read German, or can make his way about in that language with the aid of a dictionary, the three volumes of the Kretzschmar *Führer durch den Konzertsaal* are splendid sources of additional ideas for suitable program material. Volume I discusses in detail symphonies and suites from Gabrieli to Schumann; volume II, from Berlioz to the present; volume III, the entire history of the instrumental concerto in all its forms.

A word of caution must be expressed regarding research in the field of unfamiliar music: great care must be exercised in choosing works for performance, for all that glitters here is not necessarily gold. There is no valid artistic point in the indiscriminate performance of unfamiliar music just because it has not been done in modern times. The mania for the first performance has no place in the amateur field. Archaeological significance is not enough. The music chosen must be of the highest standards if it is to prove stimulating and interesting to the players and to the listeners. The conductor must resist being swayed by unimportant considerations of novelty or historical interest to the exclusion of musical values. Failure to resist such considerations will undermine, and ultimately defeat, the whole purpose of finding a unique field and outlet for the amateur orchestra which will, at the same time, satisfy the orchestra's natural desire for artistic growth.

Most publishers have heretofore been disinclined to bring out scores and orchestral parts of music off the beaten track because of a lack of confidence in the existence of a sufficient market for them. A beginning has recently been made, however, by such discriminating and enterprising publishers as the Music Press Incorporated and Broude Brothers, both of New York; E. C. Schirmer, of Boston; and the Oxford University Press. These firms have published a well-chosen selection of works from the earliest period of instrumental music to the present day, in all forms and for all combinations of instruments. The composers represented include Bach, Handel, Gabrieli, Pergolesi, Vivaldi, Gretry, Rameau, Mozart, Haydn, Schubert, and many others.

A representative number of these works are carefully crosscued by the editors in such a way that they may be played as originally scored by the composer or by orchestras lacking the particular instrumentation required. Here, as in the case of unpublished works, the conductor can be his own editor and provide additional parts for any instruments at his disposal that are not called for in the score.

Publishers other than those listed above have brought out material in this field, but the few mentioned have made the most significant contributions to date. There is a great opportunity for conductors of amateur orchestras to encourage this much needed refreshing of the orchestral repertory by utilizing on their programs the publications now available. Such support would inevitably lead to the publication of a wider variety of orchestral works.

The enterprising conductor can further heighten the musical interest of his programs by doing research of his own in the field of manuscript music. Most of the major public libraries and many of the college and university libraries possess fine collections of manuscript orchestral music which can be made readily available through the medium of the photostat or of microfilm. The conductor who is trained in orchestration can, if need be, tailor this music to the requirements of his own group. If he is able to investigate the resources of libraries abroad, he will find even more unexploited material waiting to be discovered. A note in Volume I of the Kretzschmar series on Gluck's ballet-pantomime *Don Juan* led me to do research in Paris and London into the first performances of the work in these two capitals. Since only the barest outlines of the choreography have been preserved, this meant an extensive search in contemporary newspapers and magazines for reviews of the first performances. It also involved a search for the original score that led from the British Museum to the libraries of the Paris Conservatory and of the Paris Opera. With the help of photostatic and microfilm copies of all the material found, the Wellesley College Orchestra and Dance Group were able to stage a successful performance of the work in the spring of 1937. The production was not only of considerable historical interest, since it represented an art form little known in modern times, but was of decided musical worth as well. A suite of dances from the ballet has since been performed as a concert number.

A whole volume could be written about music of this sort waiting to be unearthed, but it would be unfair to deprive the individual conductor of the thrill of making his own discoveries. The main sources, guides, and procedures outlined here will provide enough clues for use as a point of departure. The horizon will automatically broaden the further a person goes in research, as additional sources will be discovered or will suggest themselves. It will, I hope, prove more helpful to set down a few sample programs showing how unfamiliar and unpublished works can be combined with published works and the standard repertory to form an interesting and well-rounded concert. A sample repertory for a college orchestra and for a community orchestra will also be included (see Appendix).

A.   Overture to "Egmont"   Beethoven
  * Concerto for Waldhorn   Anton Rosetti
    Symphony No. 5 in B flat   Schubert
  * Christ lag in Todesbanden,
        prelude   Bach (arr.)
    Dances from "The Snow
        Maiden"   Rimsky-Korsakov

B.   Suite in D major   Bach
  * Sinfonia in G minor   Anton Rosetti
  * Six Minuets   Beethoven
  † Two Canzoni for strings   Gabrieli
    Symphony in D major, "Lon-
        don"   Haydn

C. * Musik zu einem Ritterballet   Beethoven
   * Two ayres for viols   Henry VIII
   * Concerto Grosso for flute
        and strings   A. Scarlatti
   * Andante in F sharp minor
        for strings   Purcell
     Symphony in G major, "Mil-
        itary"   Haydn

* Manuscript.   † Unfamiliar music, but published.

XII

CODA

WITHOUT a broadly conceived and soundly administered program of amateur group music in all its forms, no nation can hope to rise above the level of musical mediocrity. Classroom work in music appreciation, history, and theory provides a needed background but is not enough, by itself, to develop the larger numbers of intelligent listeners we must have in our concert halls if we are to improve standards of performance and of composition. We will never become a musical nation by having music made for us. Faithful attendance at concerts and the most dutiful listening will never change a music lover into an intelligent listener. The indispensable catalytic element is the intimate personal knowledge of great music which only comes from actually playing or singing it. The professional musician, the practicing composer, and the intelligent listener all must have the solid practical foundation for their respective roles which is obtained only from the active pursuit of amateur group music in the home, the school, and the community.

This laboratory form of instrumental music, for example, means a great many things to the young musician: supplementary training under expert guidance, increased technical facility, familiarity with the orchestral literature, the development of an ensemble sense, experience in sight reading, and an added incentive to private practice and study. In addition, it sharpens aesthetic perception and awakens the critical faculty, provides experience in the mechanics of interpretation, and may even teach the observant player how to practice efficiently on his own. For all participants, but particularly those with but a modest musical talent, it is the stepping-stone to a lifetime of intelligent listening—provided, of course, that the musical diet offered them is not so deficient in caloric count that they suffer from aesthetic malnutrition throughout their adult lives. Last, but far from least, amateur instrumental music should be the medium through which the embryonic composer learns the fundamentals of practical orchestration, either by actual participation or through observation at rehearsals.

The Secondary School

Music education in general, and instrumental music in particular, has made great progress during the last two decades. Unfortunately, this progress has not been uniform either in the various phases of music education or in geographical areas. The standards of the music performed have greatly improved throughout the country, and there has been a tremendous growth of interest everywhere in bands and choruses. At the same time, ear training has lagged far behind, and the school orchestra has lost ground. Here and there one finds excellent provisions for playing and listening to chamber music, but as a general rule this important form of instrumental training is widely neglected. It is the exception to the rule to find a secondary school interested in discovering a talent for composition and equipped to offer that talent elementary theoretical training. No matter where a teacher or conductor may go, he will find opportunities either to initiate, improve, or broaden the musical facilities of the secondary school. A fine beginning has been made in this field, but we must not lose sight of the fact that it is only a beginning.

Take, for example, chamber music. The whole base of this important form of ensemble playing must be broadened at the secondary level, if only for the purpose of counteracting the present appalling lack of music making in the home. This is fast becoming a lost art in America because of the insidious encroachment of radio and television on the family circle. The orchestral conductor can help by forming chamber music groups of both winds and strings from among the members of his orchestra; by enlisting the active support of adult players in the community in sponsoring additional opportunities for students to play chamber music in various homes; and, indirectly, by urging school authorities to develop chamber music concerts for the entire student body. The effort required to launch such a venture will pay large dividends to the cause of amateur music and to the orchestra itself. Sponsorship of string quartets, for example, not only provides additional technical and ensemble experience for the players, but it will also stimulate interest in stringed instruments and help to correct the present alarming shortage of string players. This situation has been bothering colleges and conservatories for some years now, and concern has lately been expressed by conductors of major professional symphony orchestras. Apart from these immediate considerations, an early introduction to chamber music means a gift to the instrumental player of a form of music he can enjoy the rest of his life.

As a supplement to the applied music services of the secondary school, there is a great need for more summer music camps where students can combine a vacation with an opportunity to experience the finest type of intensive musical training possible. There are a few camps of this sort scattered about the country, but there are not nearly enough of them to take care of those qualified and eager to benefit from the great advantages they have to offer. Here, again, is a chance for the orchestral conductor to take the initiative.

These various phases of instrumental training, if properly fostered and developed, will greatly increase the efficiency of the applied music program at the secondary level and result in the production of well-grounded students far better prepared than they are at present to undertake the more advanced work of the college and the conservatory. Technical proficiency and ensemble experience are not, by themselves, enough. The ultimate goal in secondary school music education will only be reached when there is a universal recognition of the importance of ear training as an indispensable part of the educational program. More intensive work needs to be done in the elementary school as well as the secondary school. Ear training should be required of all students taking part in instrumental or choral groups or studying an instrument privately. At the present time almost every applicant for admission to a conservatory performs satisfactorily, or even brilliantly, at his audition; but altogether too many of these same applicants are unable to pass a rudimentary examination in music fundamentals. Needless to say, the musical development of such students is retarded because the conservatory must take the time to supply the deficiencies of their early training.

Although some of the matters just discussed may seem to be outside the scope of the instrumental conductor's primary interest, they should be of immediate concern to him for they vitally affect the extent of the contribution he can make to his students and the caliber of the results he can produce with them. He cannot afford to become so preoccupied with his own specialty that he neglects to assume leadership in correcting the deficiencies or weaknesses which may exist in these closely interrelated phases of music education.

The College

The development of extracurricular group music in the college is hampered by several factors: (1) the amount of academic work now required of the individual, which has increased by leaps and bounds over the past decade; (2) the increased emphasis placed on examinations and grades; (3) in colleges not giving credit toward the bachelor's degree for participation in group music, the necessity for the orchestra to compete with other activities for the student's free time. It is usually further handicapped by its relation to the academic community which is, at best, morganatic. Music is still classed as a "luxury" item, and while facilities for it are universally available, there is little real understanding of its value or place in the educative process. College music groups are quite often on the defensive because the academic measuring stick applied to them is a purely utilitarian one.

The contributions the college orchestra can make to the development of its membership and to the community in general have already been covered in an earlier chapter. Two other topics remain to be discussed here: (1) cooperative projects with other college activities; (2) closer liaison with the work of the music department.

From time to time over the four-year undergraduate period, the orchestra should foster coöperative projects involving the allied arts for the purpose of enriching the musical background of all the students involved and of broadening the artistic scope of their experience and training. The orchestral player needs to become familiar with the masterpieces of choral literature by means of joint concerts with the glee club. If there is a dance group on campus, he should have the opportunity to come in contact with what is being done in this important art form through the medium of at least one joint program. Each four years should be climaxed by a large-scale coöperative project involving the orchestra, the glee club, the dramatic society, and possibly the art department and the dance group, in the production of an opera or an operetta.* In many colleges, this is standard procedure, and on an annual rather than an occasional basis. It is suggested here only for the guidance of conductors who may find themselves working under different conditions. Such a long-range program of concerts and projects is not only of incalculable musical value to the amateur who participates, but it also makes a maximum artistic contribution to the college and to the community in which it is located. Its value in breaking down the sometimes excessive self-sufficiency of the various arts needs no elaboration.

All college amateur music groups should work in the closest possible coöperation with the music department. In physics, the work of the classroom is supplemented by that of the laboratory. There should be a parallel relationship in the field of music. The presentation of programs of rare and seldom heard music as a service to courses in history and appreciation has already been

* As examples of this within my own experience: Gilbert and Sullivan's "Princess Ida"; Gluck's "Alceste" and "Don Juan," at Wellesley College; and Blow's "Venus and Adonis"; Purcell's "Dido and Aeneas" and Randall Thompson's "Solomon and Balkis," at Harvard.

suggested. The orchestra can also serve the student in composition or orchestration by giving him periodic opportunities to hear his own work played. It can also provide him with practical instrumental experience by means of actual participation in the work of the orchestra, if he is qualified, or through close observation of the various instruments in action at rehearsals. This phase of the training of an American student of composition is scandalously neglected, for he seldom gets nearer an actual orchestral instrument than a textbook on orchestration or a professionally illustrated lecture.

The intimate contact with chamber music begun in high school (or earlier!) needs to be continued throughout the college period. It is not enough for the music department to offer a quartet-in-residence without supplementing it with a comprehensive program of chamber music playing and coaching for the student. Otherwise the quartet becomes a mere matter of window-dressing and kudos for the department, thereby strengthening the "luxury" suspicion previously mentioned. Student chamber music can make a fine contribution to the cultural life of the college by bringing prepared programs to the student body in the informal atmosphere of the classroom, the dormitory, the fraternity, or the sorority. At one time, Wellesley College had seven string quartets in training, ranging from several groups of beginners to a senior quartet that had been working together for four years. Five of these groups gave a total of twenty-one concerts in one season, playing in different dormitories after dinner on faculty nights or after Sunday luncheon. It has been my experience that chamber music, for the listener, is an acquired taste—like eating artichokes. It is best encouraged, at least initially, away from the formal atmosphere of the concert hall.

To supplement the college program for the amateur, there should be more opportunities for working in applied music at summer schools specifically planned to meet his needs, which are quite different from those of the would-be professional. The offerings should include chorus, orchestra, and chamber music; private instruction in applied music; class work in ear training; and a collegium musicum similar to the one so ably directed by Paul Hindemith during one of the early seasons of the Berkshire Music Center. The importance of such a summer school program lies in the fact that it enables the amateur to work much more intensively in music than he possibly can while coping with the heavy academic demands of the regular college year.

The Community

The function of the community music group in serving the general listening public and in augmenting its musical knowledge and perception has already been outlined. It also makes a contribution to the cause of amateur music by enabling adults, both with and without a college background, to continue to enjoy group music making, and by offering an additional ensemble opportunity to qualified young students. Many of our community orchestras are not content to give concerts in their home cities or towns alone, but are taking to the road to bring living music to surrounding areas. No finer service is being rendered to American music at the present time. More community orchestras should do it!

The conductors of these orchestras should take the lead in encouraging chamber music among the membership at the point where the schools and colleges leave off. They can also be of invaluable assistance to the conductors of elementary and secondary school groups in stimulating interest in orchestral instruments and in orchestral music. The closer the coöperation between the community and the school, the healthier the state of amateur music.

The cumulative effect of each of these successive steps in the training and music education of the amateur should be a tremendous increase in the number of intelligent and informed listeners supporting the activities of the professional musician. In the last analysis, it is these listeners who will determine the musical future of America. Their intolerance of inferior music and of mediocre performance of good music will, in time, raise standards of programming, of performance, and ultimately of composition. The influence of informed amateurs is needed in every nook and cranny of American music: the home, the school, the church, the community, the concert hall, the opera house, radio, and television. The more demanding they are, the higher musical standards will go.

Conductors who work with amateurs must do their level best to lift them out of the atmosphere of apologetic dilettantism in which they have worked for too long a time. Make them aware of their potentialities and, even more important, of their responsibilities in setting, maintaining, and improving musical standards. Your work with amateurs in music is neither a job nor a career. It is a crusade.

APPENDIX

APPENDIX

A Partial List of Works Performed by the Harvard University Orchestra, 1933 to 1942

(s.r.) Sight-reading evening music.
(MS) Performed from manuscript parts.
(arr.) An original arrangement for orchestra, or an expansion of an existing orchestration.

BACH, J. S.: Brandenburg Concerto No. 3 in G
    Brandenburg Concerto No. 5 in D
    Klavier Concerto in D minor
    Klavier Concerto in F minor
    Klavier Concerto in E major
    Concerto in D minor for 2 Violins
    Chorales: "Christ lag in Todesbanden" (arr.)
      "O grosser Gott von Macht" (arr.)
      "Freu dich sehr, O meine Seele" (arr.)
      "Break Forth O Beauteous Heavenly Light" (arr.)
      "Wachet auf, ruft uns die Stimme" (arr.)
      "Dein ist allein die Ehre" (arr.)
      "Wir glauben all in einem Gott" (arr.)
    Cantatas: No. 11: "Praise to God on high" (chorus)
      No. 54: "Wiederstehe doch der Sunde" (chorus)
    Magnificat (chorus)
    Sonatine from Cantata 106
    Concerto from Cantata 142
    Jesu Joy of Man's Desiring (Arr.)
    Prelude to "Wir danken Dir, Gott"
    Sinfonia to "Die Elenden sollen essen"
    Gavotte and Musette from the 3rd English Suite (arr.)
    Suite in B minor
BALLENTINE: Variations on "Mary Had A Little Lamb"

BARTOK: Three Rumanian Folk Dances
BEETHOVEN: Symphony No. 1 in C major
    Symphony No. 2 in D major (s.r.)
    Symphony No. 4 in B flat major (s.r.)
    Symphony No. 5 in C minor (s.r.)
    Symphony No. 6 in F major (s.r.)
    Symphony No. 7 in A major
    Overture to "Egmont"
    Overture to "Coriolanus" (s.r.)
    Overture to "Prometheus"
    Six German Dances
    Musik zu Einem Ritterballet (MS)
    Scherzo from Wind-trio (arr.)
    Piano Concerto No. 4 in G major
BERLIOZ: Hungarian March from "Damnation of Faust"
BLOCH: Concerto Grosso for Piano and Strings
BRAHMS: Symphony No. 1 in C minor (s.r.)
    Symphony No. 2 in D major (s.r.)
    Symphony No. 4 in E minor (s.r.)
    Hungarian Dances in G minor and D major
    "Ave Maria" for Women's Voices and Orchestra
    Variations on a Theme of Haydn (s.r.)
BUXTEHUDE: Chaconne in E minor (arr.)
CHERUBINI: Overture to "The Water Carrier"
CIMAROSA: Overture to "The Secret Marriage"
    Choruses from "The Secret Marriage": "O che gioja"
    "Per imbrogliar la testa"
CORELLI: Concerto Grosso in D major for strings
    Pastorale from "The Christmas Concerto"
DEBUSSY: Blessed Damozel, Women's Chorus and Orchestra
    Petite Suite (s.r.)
DELANEY: Night, mixed voices, piano, strings (MS)
    Work 22 (MS)
DE FALLA: Spanish Dance from "La Vida Breve"
FAURÉ: Suite from "Pelleas and Melisande"
FRANCK: Symphony in D minor (s.r.)
FRESCOBALDI: Fugue in G minor (arr.)

GABRIELI, G.: Sonata "Pian e forte," for brass instruments
Canzoni per sonar a quattro, for strings
GLAZOUNOV: Interludium in modo antico (arr.)
GLUCK: Overture to "Iphigenia in Aulis"
"Iphigenia in Tauris," selections with mixed Chorus
GLINKA: Jota Aragonesa
GRÉTRY: Overture to "Le Rival Confident" (MS)
Overture to "Le Magnifique" (MS)
GRIEG: Two pieces for Strings: "Herzwunden": "Der Früh-
ling"
Norwegian Dances, Opus 35
HANDEL: Organ Concerto in B flat major
Fireworks Music
Concerto Grosso in B minor
Concerto Grosso in F major
"Messiah," selections with mixed chorus
Overture to "Ottone" (MS)
Water Music
HAYDN: Symphony No. 1 in E flat "Drum Roll"
Symphony No. 2 in D major "London"
Symphony No. 4 in D major "Clock"
Symphony No. 6 in G major "Surprise"
Symphony No. 11 in G "Military" (s.r.)
Toy Symphony
HELM: Suite for Small Orchestra (MS)
HINDEMITH: Five Pieces for Strings
The Hunter Rides Through the Green Wood
Trauermusik for Viola and Strings
KERN: Selections from "Show Boat"
LA RUE: Concertino for Clarinet and Orchestra (MS)
LECUONA: Malaguena
MACDOWELL: Piano Concerto No. 2 in D minor
MC BRIDE: Fugato on a Well-known Theme
MENDELSSOHN: "Fingal's Cave" Overture
Scherzo from "Midsummer Night's Dream" (s.r.)
Nocturne from "Midsummer Night's Dream" (s.r.)
Overture to "Midsummer Night's Dream"

MOZART: Symphony in C major (k.338)
Symphony in D major (k.385) "Haffner"
Symphony in E flat (k.543)
Symphony in G minor (k.550)
Symphony in C major (k.551) "Jupiter"
Eine kleine Nachtmusik
A Musical Joke (k.522)
Overture to "Don Giovanni"
Overture to "The Magic Flute"
Concerto for Clarinet and Orchestra
Sonata in B flat for Organ and Strings
Masonic Funeral Music, men's voices and orchestra
Concerto in E flat for Piano
Concerto in A major for Piano
Concerto in E flat for two pianos
Serenade No. 6
Serenade Notturno for Double String Orchestra and
Tympani
MORLEY: Ayre in G minor for Strings (MS)
LEWIS: Prelude on A Southern Folk-hymn Tune "O Won-
drous Love" (MS)
PALESTRINA: Ricercari
PERGOLESI: Stabat Mater for women's voices and Strings
PEZEL: Turm musik for brass instruments (MS)
PORTER: Incidental Music to "Anthony and Cleopatra"
(MS)
PURCELL: Andante in F sharp minor for strings (MS)
Dance Suite for Flute and Strings
PROKOFIEV: Classical Symphony (s.r.)
March from "Peter and the Wolf"
RACHMANINOFF: Piano Concerto in C minor
RAVEL: Trois Chansons (arr.)
Pavane pour une enfante defunte
Minuet from The Sonatine (arr.)
RIMSKY-KORSAKOV: Dance of Clowns and March from "The
Snow Maidens"
ROSSINI: Overture to "Semiramide" (s.r.)

SCARLATTI, A.: Concerto Grosso in G minor for flute and
strings (MS)

SCHUBERT: Symphony No. 4 in C minor "Tragic"
Symphony No. 5 in B flat
Symphony No. 8 in B minor "Unfinished"

SCHUMANN: Piano Concerto in A minor

SHOSTAKOVITCH: Polka from "The Golden Age"

SIBELIUS: Valse Triste

STRAUSS, J.: Tales from The Vienna Woods
Three Choruses from "La Reine Indigo"

STRAUSS, R.: Waltzes from "Der Rosenkavalier"

SMETANA: Dances from "The Bartered Bride"

TSCHAIKOVSKY: Symphony No. 5 in E minor (s.r.)
Symphony No. 6, Alegretto grazioso
Danse Russe from the Nutcracker Suite
Sleeping Beauty Waltz

VIVALDI: Concerto for String Orchestra in G minor

VAUGHAN-WILLIAMS: Darest thou now, o soul   Choral acc.
Let us now praise famous men   Choral acc.
Magnificat, women's voices and orchestra

WAGNER: March from "Tannhauser"
Overture to "Die Meistersinger" (s.r.)
Prelude to "Lohengrin"
Prelude to "Lohengrin" Act III

WOOD: Suite for Strings (MS)
Winter Winds, women's voices and strings (MS)

New England Conservatory Orchestra, Partial Repertoire
1945–1950

BACH, C. P. E.: Concerto in D Major for orchestra

BACH, J. C.: Sinfonia in B flat
Sinfonia in D major for double orchestra

BACH, J. S.: Sonatina from the Cantata "God's Time Is Best"

BARBER: Adagio for Strings
First Essay for Orchestra

BEETHOVEN: Symphony No. 4, in B flat major, op. 60
Symphony No. 8 in F major

BENJAMIN, ARTHUR: Overture to an Italian Comedy
BERLIOZ: Minuet and March from The Damnation of Faust
    Overture, "Benvenuto Cellini"
BRAHMS: Variations on a Theme by Haydn
    Overture, Tragic
    Symphony No. 2 in D major
    Symphony No. 4 in E minor
    Overture, Academic Festival
BRUCKNER: Mass in E minor
CHERUBINI: Overture, Medea
COPLAND, AARON: An Outdoor Overture
COUPERIN-MILHAUD: Overture and Allegro from "La Sultane"
DEBUSSY: Aria from "L'Enfant Prodigue": "L'année en vain
    chasse l'année"
    Symphonic Excerpts from "Le Martyr de Saint
    Sebastien"
    Songs:
    "C'est l'extase langoureuse"
    "Il pleure dans mon coeur" (orchestrated by Wallace
    Goodrich) (MS)
DIAMOND, DAVID: Rounds for Strings
    Music for Romeo and Juliet
DOHNANYI: Variations on a Nursery Rhyme for pianoforte
and orchestra
DVORAK: Overture, "Carneval"
    Overture, "Othello"
FAURÉ: Ballade for pianoforte and orchestra
    Fantasie for pianoforte and orchestra
FRANCK, CESAR: Le Chasseur Maudit
GABRIELI, GIOVANNI: Sonata Pian e Forte for double brass
orchestra
GLAZOUNOV: Symphony in B flat, No. 5
GOLDMARK, CARL: Overture, "Sakuntala"
    Overture, "In the Spring"
HANDEL: Concerto No. 1 in G minor for organ and orchestra
    Suite from "The Faithful Shepherd" (orch. Beecham)
    Concerto Grosso in C major, No. 7 (orch. Mottl)

Water Music

Concerto Grosso in D minor, for strings, Op. 6, No. 10

HASSE, JOHANN: Psalm LI, Miserere (1728) in C minor, for chorus and orchestra

HAYDN: Overture, "L'Isola Disabitata" (1799)

Symphony in D Major, No. 5 (London Set)

Sinfonie Concertante for violin, violoncello, oboe, bassoon, and orchestra, Op. 84

HONEGGER, ARTHUR: Symphonic Psalm: King David, for narrator, soli, chorus, and orchestra

KOHS, ELLIS B.: Concerto for Orchestra (MS)

LISZT: Les Preludes

MC KINLEY, CARL: Concert Overture (MS)

MENDELSSOHN: Symphony No. 5 in D major, "Reformation"

MOZART: Concerto in E flat (K.271) for pianoforte and orchestra

Concerto in E flat (K.447) for French horn and orchestra

Concerto in B flat major for pianoforte and orchestra (K.450)

Overture, "Die Entfuhrung aus dem Serail"

Overture, "The Marriage of Figaro"

Overture, "Cosi fan tutti"

Overture, "Der Schauspieldirektor"

Sinfonia Concertante in E flat for oboe, clarinet, horn, bassoon, and orchestra (K.297b)

Serenade in C minor (K.388)

Regina Coeli, for chorus and orchestra (K.108)

PEZEL: Tower Music for brass instruments (MS)

PISTON: Prelude and Allegro for organ and strings

Concerto for Orchestra

PROCTER, LELAND: Symphony No. 1 (MS)

PURCELL: Suite for flute and strings

RAWSTHORNE, ALAN: Street Corner Overture (MS)

RESPIGHI: Suite of Ancient Dances and Airs for the Lute from the sixteenth century

SCHUBERT: Symphony No. 3 in D major
    Symphony No. 4 in C minor, "Tragic"
SCHUMANN: Symphony in D minor, No. 4
    Symphony in E flat major, No. 3 ("Rhenish"), Op. 97
STRAUSS, RICHARD: Trio and duet from Der Rosenkavalier, Act III
    Suite from "Le bourgeois gentilhomme"
VIVALDI: Concerto in G minor for string orchestra
    Concerto in D minor for orchestra
WALTON: Overture to "Scapino"
WAGNER: Wotan's Farewell and Magic Fire Music, from Die Walkure, Act III
    Siegfried's Rhine Journey from Götterdammerung
    Excerpts from Act III "Die Meistersinger"
    Forging of the Sword, "Siegfried"
    Prelude to Act III, Lohengrin
WILLIAMS, VAUGHAN: Variants of "Dives and Lazarus" for strings and harps
    Concerto for oboe and strings
    Fantasia on Greensleeves
WOLF-FERRARI: Overture, "The Secret of Suzanne"